THE BIRD-WATCHER'S GUIDE
TO THE WETLANDS OF BRITAIN

THE BIRD-WATCHER'S GUIDE TO THE WETLANDS OF BRITAIN

M. A. Ogilvie

B. T. Batsford Ltd, London

First published 1979
© M. A. Ogilvie 1979

ISBN 0 7134 0847 2

Typeset by Bristol Typesetting Co. Ltd,
Barton Manor, St. Philips, Bristol,
Printed and bound in Great Britain
by Redwood-Burn Ltd,
London, Trowbridge & Esher,
for the publisher
B. T. Batsford Ltd,
4 Fitzhardinge Street, London W1H 0AH

Contents

List of maps

List of illustrations

(Between pages 96 and 97)

Acknowledgements

To provide the tables of the numbers of wildfowl and waders which occur at each haunt I have drawn on two main sources. The information on wildfowl came from the files of the Wildfowl Trust, in particular those of the National Wildfowl Count Scheme, and that on waders from the Birds of Estuaries Enquiry, run jointly by the British Trust for Ornithology, the Royal Society for the Protection of Birds and the Wildfowl Trust. The respective organizers, George Atkinson Willes and Tony Prater, were most helpful in giving me access to the files and generally answering my queries. The Nature Conservancy Council, the Natural Environment Research Council and the Institute of Terrestrial Ecology gave permission for use of the Wildfowl Count and Birds of Estuaries Enquiry data which were gathered in the course of work financed by contracts between those bodies and the Wildfowl Trust and the British Trust for Ornithology. My grateful thanks are due to all concerned in helping me in this and other ways. I should add that the way in which I have used the count data and any interpretation I have put on it is entirely my own responsibility.

The author and publisher would also like to thank Pamela Harrison for the black and white photographs in this book.

How to use the guide

The main text of the book is divided between England, Wales and Scotland, and within those countries into alphabetical order of counties or regions. The localities in each county or region are also listed alphabetically.

To extract the best value from a visit to a locality it is advantageous to possess the relevant 1:50,000 Ordnance Survey sheet, the number of which is given against each locality. Also given is a two-letter, four-figure grid reference which will pinpoint the wetland more precisely. Note that many smaller-scale maps and readily available road atlases also show the National Grid lines.

For each wetland fully described in the text, details are given of access, both the main roads to be taken, and, where appropriate, tracks and footpaths. In all cases, footpaths mentioned have been checked against the current Ordnance Survey 1:50,000 maps as being public Rights of Way. However their presence on the OS maps, and therefore mention in this book, does not guarantee their existence on the ground and bird-watchers should not attempt to use this book as evidence of a Right of Way where a path has been obstructed, diverted or abolished.

Some of the wetlands described are reserves, either National Nature Reserves, or ones owned by the Royal Society for the Protection of Birds, the Wildfowl Trust, or other voluntary body. At some, though not all, permits are required for access, though at others it is possible to see as much as one wants from public roads or public hides, or sometimes, as in the case of Wildfowl Trust reserves, by payment of a small fee on the spot. For permits to visit National Nature Reserves write, in the first instance, to The Nature Conservancy Council, 19 Belgrave Square, London, SW1X 8PY, though these are normally only given for serious scientific study; and for RSPB reserves, to the Royal Society for the Protection of Birds, The Lodge, Sandy, Bedfordshire, SG19 2DL, or to the address given in the detailed account.

Sites which are not described in detail may, in some cases, be privately owned or have restricted access and intending bird-watchers should obtain the necessary permission before visiting them.

12

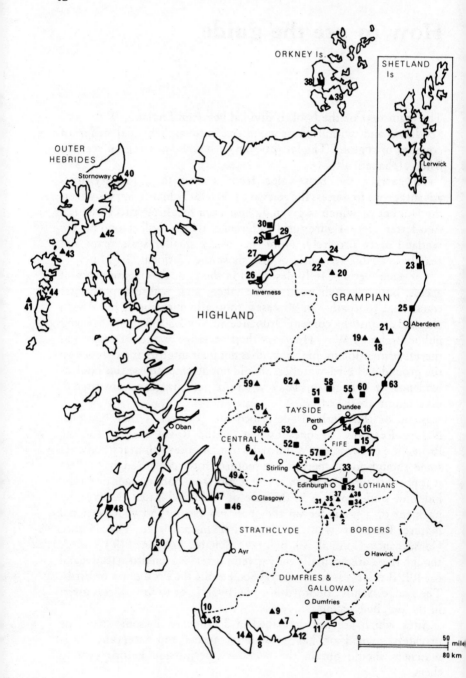

SCOTLAND

Borders
 1. Baddinsgill Res.
 2. Portmore Res.
 3. Westwater Res.

Central
 4. Flanders Moss
 5. Gartmorn Dam
 6. Lake of Menteith

Dumfries & Galloway
 7. Carlingwark Loch
 8. Fleet Bay
 9. Loch Ken
 10. Loch Ryan
 11. NORTH SOLWAY
 12. Rough Firth
 13. Stranraer Lochs
 14. Wigtown Bay

Fife
 15. CAMERON RES.
 16. EDEN ESTUARY
 17. KILCONQUHAR LOCH

Grampian
 18. Dee Valley floods
 19. Lochs Davan & Kinnord
 20. Loch Park
 21. Loch of Skene
 22. Loch Spynie
 23. LOCH OF STRATHBEG
 24. Speymouth
 25. YTHAN ESTUARY

Highland
 26. BEAULY & INNER MORAY FIRTHS
 27. CROMARTY FIRTH
 28. DORNOCH FIRTH
 29. LOCH EYE
 30. LOCH FLEET

Lothians
 31. Cobbinshaw Res.
 32. DUDDINGSTON LOCH
 33. FIRTH OF FORTH
 34. GLADHOUSE RES.
 35. Harperrig Res.
 36. Rosebery Res.
 37. Threipmuir Res.

Orkney
 38. LOCHS OF HARRAY & STENNESS
 39. Scapa Flow

Outer Hebrides
 40. Broad Bay
 41. Monach Isles
 42. Shiant Isles
 43. Sound of Harris
 44. Uists & Benbecula

Shetland
 45. Loch Spiggie

Strathclyde
 46. CASTLE SEMPLE LOCH
 47. Firth of Clyde
 48. ISLAY
 49. Loch Lomond
 50. Mull of Kintyre

Tayside
 51. BLAIRGOWRIE LOCHS
 52. CARSEBRECK PONDS
 53. Drummond Pond
 54. FIRTH OF TAY
 55. Forfar Loch
 56. Loch Earn
 57. LOCH LEVEN
 58. LOCHS OF LINTRATHEN & KINNORDY
 59. Loch Rannoch
 60. LOCHS OF RESCOBIE & BALGAVIES
 61. Loch Tay
 62. Loch Tummel
 63. MONTROSE BASIN

■ major site ▲ minor site

14

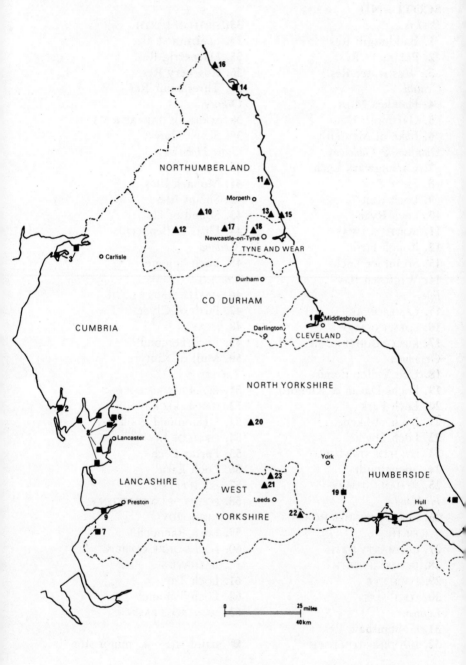

NORTHUMBERLAND

▲16

■14

▲11

Morpeth ○

▲10

▲12   ▲17   ▲13 ▲15

▲18

Newcastle-on-Tyne ○

○ Carlisle

■3

TYNE AND WEAR

Durham ○

CO DURHAM

CUMBRIA

1 ■

Middlesbrough ○

Darlington ○

CLEVELAND

NORTH YORKSHIRE

▲20

■2

■6

York ○

8

○ Lancaster

HUMBERSIDE

LANCASHIRE

▲23

▲21

WEST

19 ■

○ Preston

Leeds ○

5 ■

Hull

4 ■

YORKSHIRE

22 ▲

■9

■7

0   25 miles
▭▭▭▭▭▭▭▭
40 km

NORTHERN ENGLAND

Cleveland
1. TEESMOUTH

Cumbria
2. DUDDON ESTUARY
3. SOUTH SOLWAY

Humberside
4. HORNSEA MERE
5. HUMBER ESTUARY

Lancashire
6. LEIGHTON MOSS
7. MARTIN MERE
8. MORECAMBE BAY
9. RIBBLE ESTUARY

Northumberland
10. Colt Crag & Hallington Res.
11. Cresswell Ponds
12. Greenlee & Broomlee Res.

13. Holywell Ponds
14. LINDISFARNE
15. Seaton Sluice
16. Tweed Estuary
17. Whittledene Res.

Tyne & Wear
18. Gosforth Park Lake

North Yorkshire
19. DERWENT FLOODS
20. Gouthwaite Res.

West Yorkshire
21. Eccup Res.
22. Fairburn Ings
23. Harewood Park Lake

■ major site   ▲ minor site

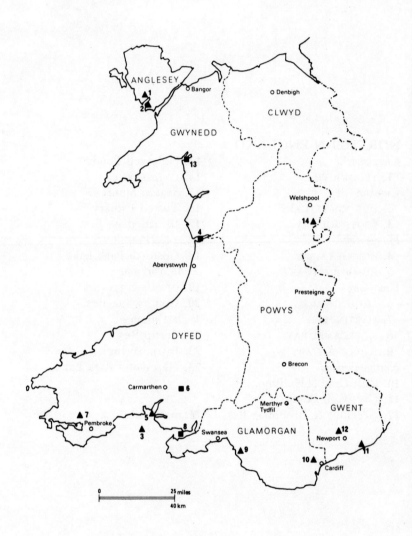

WALES
Anglesey
 1. Llyn Coron
 2. Malltraeth Bay
Dyfed
 3. Carmarthen Bay
 4. DYFI ESTUARY
 5. Gwendraeth Estuary
 6. TOWY VALLEY
 7. Western Cleddau
Glamorgan
 8. BURRY INLET

 9. Eglwys Nunydd Res.
10. Llanishen Res.
Gwent
11. Caldicot Level
12. Llandegfedd Res.
Gwynedd
13. TRAETH BACH
Powys
14. R. Severn, Welshpool

■ major site ▲ minor site

18

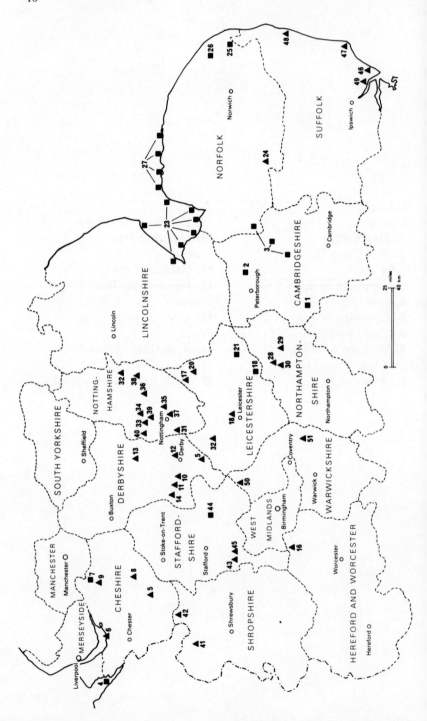

CENTRAL ENGLAND

Cambridge
1. GRAFHAM WATER
2. NENE WASHES
3. OUSE WASHES

Cheshire
4. DEE ESTUARY
5. Doddington Pool
6. Mersey Estuary
7. ROSTHERNE MERE
8. Sandbach Flashes
9. Tatton Park Mere

Derbyshire
10. Allestree Lake
11. Kedleston Lake
12. Locko Hall Lake
13. Ogston Res.
14. Osmaston Lake
15. Staunton Harold Res.

Hereford & Worcester
16. Barnt Green Res.

Leicestershire
17. Belvoir Ponds
18. Cropston & Swithland Res.
19. EYEBROOK RES.
20. Knipton Res.
21. RUTLAND WATER
22. Thornton & Blackbrook Res.

Lincolnshire
23. THE WASH

Norfolk
24. Breckland Pools
25. BREYDON WATER
26. HICKLING & HORSEY MERES

27. NORTH NORFOLK COAST

Northamptonshire
28. Hollowell Res.
29. Pitsford Res.
30. Ravensthorpe Res.

Nottinghamshire
31. Attenborough Pits
32. Besthorpe Pits
33. Carburton Lake
34. Clumber Lake
35. Gunthorpe Pits
36. Hoveringham Pits
37. Radcliffe Pits
38. South Muskham Pits
39. Thoresby Lake
40. Welbeck Lake

Shropshire
41. Ellesmere Meres
42. Whitchurch Meres

Staffordshire
43. Belvide Res.
44. BLITHFIELD RES.
45. Gailey Pools

Suffolk
46. Deben Est.
47. Havergate
48. MINSMERE & WALBERSWICK
49. Orwell Est.

Warwickshire
50. Alvecote Pools
51. Draycote Water

■ major site   ▲ minor site

20

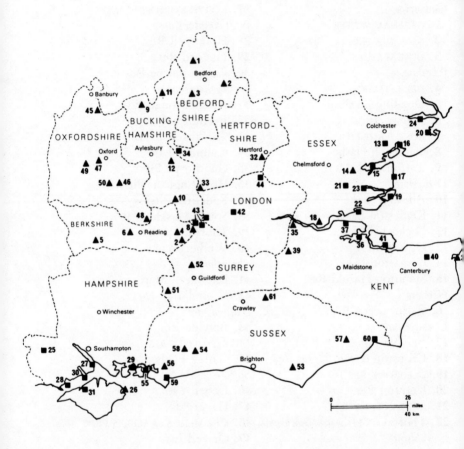

▲1
Bedford ○
▲2
Banbury ○
▲11
BEDFORD-
▲3
SHIRE
45 ▲
▲9
BUCKING-
HERTFORD-
SHIRE
Colchester ○
24 ■
OXFORDSHIRE HAMSHIRE
Aylesbury ○
ESSEX
20 ■
13 ■
Oxford ○
■ 34
Hertford ○
16 ■
47
32 ▲
49 ▲
12
Chelmsford ○
14 ▲
50 ▲ ▲ 46
▲33
15 ■
17 ■
21 ■
23 ■
19 ■
▲ 10
LONDON
48
44 ■
22 ■
BERKSHIRE
43
■ 42
18 ▲
37 ■
6 ▲ Reading
▲ 4 ▲ 8
35 ▲
36 ■
▲ 5
2 ▲
39 ▲
41 ■
▲ 52
40 ■
▲ A
HAMPSHIRE
SURREY
○ Maidstone
Canterbury ○
Guildford ○
▲ 51
KENT
○ Winchester
▲ 61
Crawley ○
SUSSEX
57 ▲
60 ■
■ 25
58 ▲ ▲ 54
○ Southampton
Brighton
27
29
56 ▲
▲ 53
28
30
55
59 ■
31
▲ 26

0   25
miles
40 km

SOUTH-EAST ENGLAND

Bedfordshire
1. Felmersham Pits
2. Sandy Pits
3. Stewartby Pits

Berkshire
4. Great Meadow Pond
5. Thatcham Pits
6. Theale Pits
7. Virginia Water
8. Wraysbury Pits

Buckinghamshire
9. Foxcote Res.
10. Marlow Pits
11. Newport Pagnell Pits
12. Weston Turville Pits

Essex
13. ABBERTON RES.
14. Ardleigh Res.
15. BLACKWATER ESTUARY
16. COLNE ESTUARY
17. DENGIE PENINSULA
18. East Tilbury
19. FOULNESS ISLAND
20. HAMFORD WATER
21. HANNINGFIELD RES.
22. LEIGH MARSH
23. NORTH FAMBRIDGE
24. STOUR ESTUARY

Hampshire
25. AVON FLOODS
26. Brading Harbour
27. CALSHOT CASTLE to FAWLEY
28. KEYHAVEN & PENNINGTON MARSHES
29. LANGSTONE HARBOUR
30. NEEDS OAR POINT
31. NEWTOWN MARSH

Hertfordshire
32. Broxbourne Pits
33. Rickmansworth Pits
34. TRING RES.

Kent
35. INNER THAMES
36. MEDWAY MARSHES
37. NORTH KENT MARSHES
38. Pegwell & Sandwich Bays
39. Sevenoaks Pits
40. STODMARSH
41. THE SWALE

London
42. BARN ELMS RES.
43. DATCHET, STAINES, Q. MARY, Q.E. 2 Reservoirs
44. LEA VALLEY RES.

Oxfordshire
45. Cherwell Valley Floods
46. Dorchester Pits
47. Farmoor Res.
48. Sonning Pits
49. Standlake Pits
50. Sutton Courtenay Pits

Surrey
51. Frensham Ponds
52. Guildford Pits

Sussex
53. Arlington Res.
54. Arun Floods
55. CHICHESTER HARBOUR
56. Chichester Pits
57. Darwell Res.
58. Duncton Res.
59. PAGHAM HARBOUR
60. RYE HARBOUR
61. Weirwood Res.

■ major site ▲ minor site

22

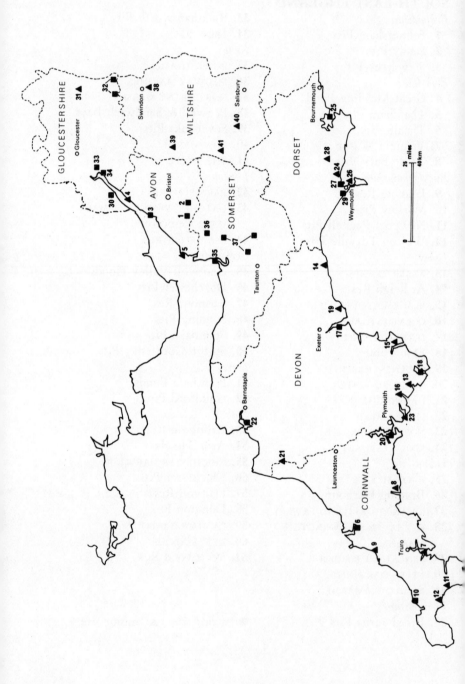

SOUTH-WEST ENGLAND

Avon
1. BLAGDON RES.
2. CHEW VALLEY LAKE
3. CHITTENING WARTH
4. Littleton
5. Sand Bay

Cornwall
6. CAMEL ESTUARY
7. Fal Estuary
8. Fowey Estuary
9. Gannel Estuary
10. HAYLE ESTUARY
11. Loe Pool
12. Marazion Marsh

Devon
13. Avon Estuary
14. Axe Estuary
15. Dart Estuary
16. Erme Estuary
17. EXE ESTUARY
18. KINGSBRIDGE ESTUARY
19. Otter Estuary
20. TAMAR ESTUARY
21. Tamar Lake
22. TAW/TORRIDGE ESTUARY

23. Yealm Estuary

Dorset
24. Lodmoor
25. POOLE HARBOUR
26. Portland Harbour
27. RADIPOLE LAKE
28. R. Frome Floods
29. THE FLEET

Gloucestershire
30. AYLBURTON WARTH
31. Bourton Pits
32. COTSWOLD WATER PARK
33. FRAMPTON POOLS
34. NEW GROUNDS

Somerset
35. BRIDGWATER BAY
36. CHEDDAR RES.
37. SOMERSET LEVELS

Wiltshire
38. Coate Water
39. Corsham Lake
40. Fonthill Lake
41. Longleat Lake

■ major site ▲ minor site

WETLANDS AND THEIR BIRDS

Wetland habitat is among the richest and most diverse of any that exist. The sheer wealth of plant and animal life that can be supported by an area in which water plays an important part is rarely equalled elsewhere. The water must, of course, be essentially fertile, and this normally means that the underlying soils and rocks are basic, not acidic. Thus natural or artificial lakes in areas of limestone or chalk will support far more life than those in areas of, for example, granite rocks or peat. Birds will sometimes use such latter waters, but only as roosts or resting places as the necessary food will be lacking. It follows, therefore, from the geology and topography of Britain that the best fresh waters for birds are those in the lowlands.

The shallow seas round the coasts of Britain are quite fertile in their own right, but where rivers have produced broad estuaries— and Britain is particularly well off for these—then the fertility of the rivers combined with that of the sea can produce exceptionally rich conditions. This habitat will support enormous numbers of birds because the underlying mud or sand itself is alive with invertebrate life. Estuarine vegetation, too, can be very important, capable of supporting huge flocks of grazing species, such as Brent Geese or Wigeon.

In the main, the temperate zone of the northern hemisphere is not nearly so attractive to birds for the purposes of breeding when those birds are dependent on water. The great majority of breeding waders and wildfowl do so in countries to the north—up to, and often well beyond the Arctic Circle. Forced to leave such areas at the onset of winter, they move south to reach regions where they can safely live for the coldest part of the year. For some species this entails a journey across the equator and into the southern hemisphere, but many more stop at the first reasonable area. The coasts of the North Sea provide one such area, and the estuaries and inland waters of Britain together make up a vital wintering range for enormous numbers of birds of many species.

As well as these birds which come to spend the winter, Britain is a stopping-off place for perhaps as many birds again on their journey further south. Our estuaries have been well described as hotels with some short-term guests, in both autumn and spring, and some longer-term visitors spending perhaps months in the one site. The large reservoirs and natural lakes perform just the same function.

Whilst it may be readily recognized that wetlands are very good habitat and attract many birds, it is another thing altogether to discover just how many birds might be involved, both at any one site and nationally. The Wildfowl Trust has been organizing counts of ducks, geese and swans for over 30 years and these have provided a fund of vital information on almost every wetland of any importance throughout the country. The basic technique is to request local bird-watchers to count the number of birds present on their local water on the middle Sunday of each month from October to March. In some areas, there is a count in September as well. Naturally the larger waters, and in particular estuaries, require a co-ordinated team, but the majority of waters are covered by just one or two people.

The very fact that there is continuity in those who count means an increased reliability in the results. One person will build up good experience of the best way to count his particular water, and if he is prone to over- or under-estimate numbers when counting, then his error is likely to be consistent. One of the principle ways in which the monthly count data is used is in the preparation of indices for the commoner species, whereby the counts for a sample of about 120 of the more important waters are compared directly with the number of birds present at those same waters in previous months or years. These indices show clearly whether populations are increasing or decreasing. An inaccurate counter, provided he is consistent, will still record changes even if his actual figures are not very precise.

Between 600 and 800 waters are covered regularly by the monthly wildfowl counts, but for most of the commoner species this represents only a proportion of their estimated total population in the country. A better idea of actual total populations has come from international wildfowl counts held once or twice a winter, when counters are asked to cover every water possible and not just their regular ones. These counts are now carried out throughout much of Europe and further afield and are beginning to provide good information on regional populations as well as individual country totals.

For the majority of the goose species wintering in Britain, it has proved possible to carry out complete censuses. A few such censuses are made at least annually, but less regular counts have to be accepted for more widespread or difficult populations. Again, amateur bird-watchers are usually involved, and indeed much of the work could not be carried out without their assistance. The Greylag and Pink-footed Geese are censused together over one weekend in early November each year with the help of up to 100 local counters. Their range overlaps considerably at that time of year and they are concentrated into relatively few haunts. Later on in the winter they become much more spread out and attempts at late winter censuses have produced unsatisfactory results.

Swans in Britain present varied counting problems. The Bewick's and the Whooper both occur in Ireland as well and the paucity of counters there makes complete counts harder to achieve, especially as there is considerable movement between the two countries. The Mute Swan has been censused at intervals, but tends to receive less attention than its 'wild' relatives.

While the wildfowl have been regularly counted in Britain for up to 30 years in some cases, waders were almost completely ignored until much more recently. Then, in the late 1960s, a pilot study showed that it was feasible to count all the waders in an estuary, even such a large and difficult one as Morecambe Bay. There was then launched the Birds of Estuaries Enquiry, supported by the three major ornithological organizations in the country. The coverage has been very good indeed and monthly counts almost throughout the year have been achieved for many localities. The numbers of some species surprised many people, especially when it became apparent that Britain was holding significant proportions of the total populations in Europe for some species. The period of full counts within the Enquiry has now finished after five years, but the work is carrying on at a reduced scale in the form of regular monitoring.

With the addition of the figures from the Estuaries Enquiry to the Wildfowl Count data there now exists really good information on the status of all the estuaries round our coasts to go with the knowledge of the inland waters which has been available for many years. Thus it is possible to detail all the major wetlands of the country, to show which are carrying large numbers of which species, and to demonstrate their relative importance.

Wetlands, and in particular estuaries and riverside floods, seem to attract drainage and reclamation schemes, plans for barrages and pollution of all forms. The threats to these areas are growing all the time, becoming a never-ending stream. Many wetlands have been lost, others are even now being gouged away, while a whole long list are in need of constant attention to ward off or combat the attention of those who wish to use them for some purpose other than to support wildlife. Some of these are mentioned in the site accounts and, on the most pessimistic prognosis, readers of this book may expect that one or more places described as being worth visiting will have disappeared within the next few years. Britain, perhaps more than many other countries, has a number of discrete populations, or one in which the great majority occur within our shores. The conservation implications of this are obvious and make the safeguarding of our wetlands even more vital.

Bird-watchers, not surprisingly, find wetlands rewarding places to visit. Wildfowl and waders can both provide marvellous spectacles of sheer numbers, or beauty of plumage and form. Further, wetlands seem to act as magnets for rare visitors from distant lands, and this combination is probably unrivalled in any other habitat.

The scope of this book is to cover only the more important wetlands, omitting the very small estuaries, private lakes and gravel pits which, because of their limited areas, can hold only quite small numbers of birds. Diversity may be there, and bird-watching may indeed be very good, but as some selection had to take place, a combination of size and numbers was chosen.

After an introductory paragraph or two describing the area and, sometimes—briefly—the birds to be found there, details are given of how to reach the best spots from which to observe the area. The sheet number of the Ordnance Survey 1:50,000 series is given together with a grid reference for the approximate centre of the wetland. In stating how to reach each place I have assumed the use of a car and the willingness to go on foot. Where public footpaths are shown on maps I have tried to indicate this, but cannot, of course, guarantee that access will not have been barred, for whatever reason.

For some sites I have urged restraint on the part of bird-watchers, in order to prevent disturbance of the birds they have come to watch. It could be argued that by the very act of publishing this book I am encouraging more and more people to visit these threatened and easily disturbed habitats, yet it can equally well be claimed that the more people who know of and appreciate these places, the stronger will be the opposition to any proposal to spoil them. I am not, unfortunately, able to be quite certain that some bird-watchers will not go too far and disturb birds or even cause positive harm, but such minorities will always exist while the majority accept occasional limits on their activities in the knowledge that they are benefiting the birds in which they are so obviously and genuinely interested.

For nearly every site there are tables indicating the order of abundance of the various species of wildfowl, and, shown separately for estuaries, waders. The figures come from an examination of the Wildfowl Count and Birds of Estuaries results. For a small number of sites there is insufficient data to give even this amount of information.

The tabulated figures are based on the normal maximum level reached at that site, taking an average over the last five years. It should be borne in mind that peak counts at any one locality can vary quite markedly from year to year depending on local weather and water conditions, and on annual breeding success. A visit at the right time of year should, however, produce counts within the range shown. The timing of peak numbers in Britain is given below under the individual species headings. Comparing the peak figure for a particular wetland with the estimated British total enables one to assess the relative importance of individual localities to that species or population. This is shown, in percentage terms, for some of the most important waters described.

The presence of some species is not regular enough to justify in-clusion in the tables, perhaps only occurring in some years, or for only a month or two, and that rather unpredictably. I have not attempted to list every species which has been seen at each water, but have given those which a bird-watcher might reasonably be expected to see in the course of several visits. Where no figure is given against the species, the maximum ever likely to be seen will be under 100.

A detailed analysis of the Birds of Estuaries results will be appearing in book form in 1979 or 1980, while a full account of almost all British wildfowl haunts, based on Wildfowl Count data, was published in 1963 (Wildfowl in Great Britain, HMSO), and is currently being considered for revision. Many counties publish bird reports giving counts for individual sites in full.

THE SPECIES OF WATERFOWL

There follows a short section on each of the different species of waterfowl which are mentioned under the site headings. After the species name is a figure, or range of figures, which represents the estimated total British population at its annual peak, over the last five years. For a few species, notably the geese, actual counts are available, and these have been averaged for the past five years. In the text which follows a comment is made on the accuracy or otherwise of the figure, and it is usually also set in the context of north-west Europe.

Brief information is also usually given on the overall distribution of the species, and on the more detailed range within Britain. Habitat and food are covered in a sentence or two.

Mute Swan (15,000: estimate as no census since 1961)
A widespread resident but avoiding uplands much over 180 m (600 ft).
The population has declined from a peak of perhaps 20,000 in the late
1950s and may be lower than the figure given. The north-west
European population may be as high as 120,000 but apart from very
occasional hard-weather immigrants these do not come to our shores.
There are few large concentrations in Britain, with flocks of over 500
confined to a handful of far-flung sites in Dorset, the Outer Hebrides
and perhaps Essex. A vegetarian, the Mute Swan is at home on fresh
or brackish waters and occurs on many estuaries.

Whooper Swan (3,500: estimate based on available counts)
Two separate populations winter in Britain; the great majority
belong to the Iceland breeding population, with perhaps another
2,000 birds passing through to Ireland where they also winter. Small
flocks in East Anglia belong to the Scandinavian-Russian breeding
stock, which numbers up to 14,000, and which winters around the
western Baltic and in the Netherlands. Whooper Swans mostly occur
in small flocks of up to 100, though some larger groups can be seen in
the autumn soon after their arrival. They are found on the larger
lakes and some estuaries, feeding on submerged vegetation, and in a
few places the outfalls from distilleries. They arrive in Britain in late
October and leave during April.

Bewick's Swan (2,000: accurate counts)
The total population of north-west Europe is about 9,000, rather
larger than had been supposed until a recent complete census.
Numbers in Britain have grown steadily over the last 30 years or
more, with the Ouse Washes holding over 1,000 at peak. The habitat
requirement is of wet grassland—a decreasing commodity—but it
has been shown by the Wildfowl Trust that they will adapt to less
natural conditions and take supplementary food, such as grain, if
provided. They are present from October to mid-March.

Bean Goose (150: accurate counts)
The two small flocks in Britain, plus occasional stragglers, are a
remnant of former much larger numbers. The decline seems to be
connected with a desertion of Scandinavian breeding grounds. So far
there has been no spill-over from the rapidly increasing numbers of
Russian-breeding birds now wintering in the Netherlands. Bean
Geese like undisturbed areas of grazing, preferably wet meadows.
They arrive quite late in December and leave again in March.

Pink-footed Goose   (75,000: annual census of good accuracy)
The entire Iceland and East Greenland breeding population of
Pinkfeet winters within Britain, mainly in Scotland, plus a few
localities in England, including the Wash and Lancashire. There is
another, completely separate, population of about 12,000–15,000
breeding in Svalbard and wintering in the Netherlands. The British
population reached a peak of 89,000 in the early 1970s but has since
declined following some poor breeding seasons. On arrival in early
October (occasionally late September) the geese feed on barley
stubble, then move progressively on to harvested potato fields and
then grass. There is considerable movement around the country
during the winter, the birds avoiding some of the more disturbed
estuary areas until after the end of the shooting season. They depart in
mid-April.

White-fronted Goose   (10,500: annual census plus fairly complete
counts)
About 6,000 of the above figure are European Whitefronts wintering
in the southern half of England and Wales, and part of a very much
larger population breeding in Russia and mostly wintering in the
Netherlands. The other 4,500 are Greenland Whitefronts, wintering
in a few localities in Scotland and western Wales, with about another
8,000 wintering in Ireland. Both races feed on grassland, but the
European Whitefront prefers well-grazed fields, preferably wet and
splashy in winter, while the Greenland birds live more on rough
grazing land and even bog. Both races arrive in Britain in October,
but the European birds depart in mid-March, while the Greenland
birds stay until mid-April.

Greylag Goose   (65,000: annual census of good accuracy)
In a similar pattern to the Pinkfeet, the entire breeding population of
Iceland Greylags winters within Britain. Here they join perhaps 2,000
resident birds in north-west Scotland and the Hebrides, and another
one or two thousand feral birds. They arrive at the end of October
and follow a feeding cycle of barley stubble, potato fields and grass,
roosting mainly on inland waters in preference to estuaries. They
leave for Iceland in April.

Canada Goose   (20,000: censused in 1976, may have grown since)
This species is mainly one of small inland waters, such as private lakes
and gravel pits. It has not occurred much on the larger inland waters,

needing islands on which to breed, nor are they common on estuaries, although they do occur regularly on a few on the south coast. They feed on vegetation, principally on farmland. The majority of British Canada Geese are sedentary, though there is one known moult migration of non-breeding birds from North Yorkshire to the Beauly Firth, Highland Region.

Barnacle Goose   (32,000: census of one population, regular counts of the majority of the other)
There are two populations of Barnacle Geese in Britain. The whole of the Svalbard breeding population winters on the Solway Firth, the estuary dividing Scotland and England on the west coast. Here they feed on saltmarsh and adjacent pasture. The other population breeds in East Greenland and winters on islands off the west coast of Scotland and Ireland. There are about 4,000 in the latter country and 25,000 in Scotland, of which around 20,000 are on the island of Islay in the Inner Hebrides, also feeding on saltmarsh and grassland. There is a third population of about 50,000 birds breeding in the USSR and wintering in the Netherlands. The flock on Islay has increased greatly in recent years, producing a conservation problem. Local farmers are complaining of damage to crops but any measures taken against the geese must be tempered with the knowledge that no less than two-thirds of a complete population is involved, a concentration that must equally be safeguarded. Barnacle Geese arrive on the Solway at the end of September and on Islay in late October; both populations leave in mid-April.

Brent Goose   (40,000: quite accurate census in mid-winter)
The Dark-bellied Brent Goose breeds in Arctic Siberia and winters round the shores on the North Sea and in western France. The total population has increased very fast from under 30,000 ten years ago to about 90,000 in 1977–78, having reached a peak of 120,000 in 1975–76. Up to 40 per cent winter in Britain on the east and south coast where they feed on *Zostera* and *Enteromorpha* and, in recent years, on adjacent pasture and winter wheat.
  A peak of a little over 1,000 Light-bellied Brent Geese winter at Lindisfarne, Northumberland, coming from a total population of not more than 3,000 breeding in Svalbard; the remainder winter in Denmark. There are up to 15,000 Light-bellied Brent in Ireland but these are a separate population.

Shelduck   (65,000: good estimate based on fairly complete counts)
A common breeding species all round our coasts, and penetrating
inland in some areas. It has been estimated that there are about 12,000
breeding pairs in the country. The majority of the adults leave in July
to moult in the Heligoland Bight, returning from October onwards.
Peak numbers are usually reached in January or February. Shelducks
live in muddy or sandy estuaries where they sieve small molluscs from
the surface layers of mud. The British peak represents about 50 per
cent of the north-west European population.

Mallard   (300,000: not much better than an educated guess)
The Mallard is common throughout Britain, breeding over a very
wide range of habitats. In winter, too, flocks are found on all kinds
and sizes of water, taking a considerable variety of animal and plant
food. There are comparatively few large concentrations of over
2,000, and the very dispersed nature makes anything like a good
estimate of the total population almost impossible. The majority of
British breeding Mallard appear to be sedentary; they are joined each
autumn by migrants from the Continent, particularly in the eastern
half of the country. Peak numbers are usually reached early in the
autumn and counts decline thereafter.

Teal   (75,000: estimate based on fairly good counts)
There are a few thousand breeding pairs of Teal in Britain, mostly in
the northern half, but substantially larger numbers come for the
winter from breeding grounds around the Baltic. Although more
often occurring in flocks of a few hundred, one or two very large
concentrations occur of 5,000 or even more. Peak counts are usually
made in December or January. Teal use estuaries and the larger
inland waters, as well as shallow floods where they can sift the
surface layer and margins for small seeds. The estimated peak for
Britain is about half the north-west European population.

Gadwall   (2,000–3,000: estimate)
About 250 pairs of Gadwall are thought to breed in Britain, scattered
in many areas. The winter peak is reinforced by small numbers of
birds from the Continent, the picture being confused by the
introduction of hand-reared birds in several localities. Gadwall
mainly occur on inland freshwater, only occasionally on estuaries.
They have a mixed diet of insects, seeds and water plants.

Wigeon   (200,000: estimate based on actual counts of c. 150,000).
A few hundred pairs of Wigeon breed, mainly in Scotland, but the
great majority of our wintering birds come from breeding areas in
northern Scandinavia and Arctic Russia, east to at least 70°E. Some
wintering in northern Scotland also come from Iceland. Primarily an
estuarine bird, the Wigeon feeds on *Zostera* and *Enteromorpha* growing
on the mudflats, as well as grazed saltmarsh. Some inland flocks
occur, notably the largest of all, over 35,000, on the Ouse Washes,
Cambridgeshire. Some estuary flocks top 10,000. Peak numbers
generally occur between November and January when about half the
north-west European total is in Britain.

Pintail   (24,000: good estimate based on fairly complete counts)
Numbers of Pintail wintering in Britain have been increasing in
recent years, with a tendency for there to be rather a few large
concentrations, notably in the Lancashire/Cheshire estuaries. The
only inland flock of any size is on the Ouse Washes. A very small
number of pairs stay to breed but the bulk of our winter visitors come
from northern Russia. The north-west European population, of
which the British birds are part, numbers about 50,000. Pintail usually
up-end to feed in shallow water, but can also be found feeding on
autumn stubble in some areas. Peak numbers are found from October
through to February.

Shoveler   (5,000: estimate)
Shoveler are widespread in small numbers on both estuaries and
shallow inland waters where they sieve the surface with their broad
filtering bill. About 1,000 pairs breed and they and their offspring
migrate south to Iberia and France for the winter. Their place is taken
by immigrants from the Continent, from as far east as Russia. Peak
numbers actually occur in spring when both populations are present
for a time.

Pochard   (45,000: quite good estimate)
Pochard numbers have grown considerably in recent years, probably
helped by the great increase in gravel digging in England, providing
perfect habitat for them. A few hundred pairs now breed but most of
our wintering flocks come from eastern Europe and central western
Russia. There are a few large flocks, notably the 7,000 plus on the tiny
Duddingston Loch in Edinburgh. The London reservoirs, too, hold
good numbers. Pochard are diving ducks, seeking their mainly plant

food under water. The north-west European population is perhaps ten times that found in Britain.

Tufted Duck   (50,000: quite good estimate)
Like its close relative, the Pochard, the Tufted Duck has been increasing steadily in recent years, but has been more successful as a breeder, taking readily to new gravel pits. One estimate puts the number of pairs at 4,500–5,000. Additional birds join ours for the winter, coming from as far as Arctic Russia. However, our total numbers are still small compared with the 250,000 estimated for Europe. Tufted Duck are often found on the same waters as Pochard, usually freshwater but occasionally on estuaries, but they avoid competition for food by taking largely animal matter from under the water. Peak numbers are present from October to February.

Scaup   (20,000: good estimate based on fairly complete counts)
There is one very large, though decreasing, flock of Scaup in the country—in the Firth of Forth near Edinburgh—which has in the past reached over 20,000 but is now lower. Even so it represents at least three-quarters of the British total. Other flocks rarely reach more than 1,000. Icelandic and Russian birds winter in Britain though the proportions are not known. In the Firth of Forth and on the Island of Islay they feed on distillery and other outfalls, though their natural food is mainly animal, including molluscs and other life off the sea bottom. It is thought that the north-west European population may be as high as 150,000, mainly in the shallow seas of the western Baltic. Peak numbers in Britain are from December to February.

Goldeneye   (12,500: fairly good estimate)
Although small numbers of Goldeneye occur on a number of inland waters, the really big flocks are all on estuaries, in particular the Firth of Forth where several thousand are recorded. The birds come from breeding grounds in Scandinavia and Russia, but the European population is very large, at about 200,000. Goldeneye feed on bottom-living animals. Substantial numbers are present for several months, from October to March.

Eider   (60,000: a guess)
The Eider Duck breeds all round our northern shores and this distribution makes it impossible to arrive at a meaningful population figure, or to monitor changes. A few large wintering concentrations

occur in the larger Scottish firths, particularly the Forth, and off the mouth of the Tay. Eiders are fairly sedentary, making short movements up and down the coasts. They feed on a variety of marine life including molluscs and crabs.

Common Scoter   (35,000: a fairly good estimate)
There are a number of important concentrations of Common Scoter in British waters but some of these have not been properly counted. This is especially true of some summer moulting flocks. Scoters often lie well offshore and so may escape regular observation. The north-west European population is thought to number several hundred thousands. Their main food is shellfish, for which they dive in water averaging 2–4 m (6–10 ft) in depth, but occasionally down to 9 m (30 ft).

Velvet Scoter   (2,000–5,000: a fairly vague estimate)
Very recent evidence suggests there may be more Velvet Scoter in the seas off Britain than was previously thought, but those within regular sighting distance of land are not numerous. They are most often found as scattered individuals among larger flocks of Common Scoter, where they take similar foods.

Long-tailed Duck   (4,000: almost certainly an underestimate)
There are very few localities where this species can be regularly seen, yet there is evidence that, as with other sea ducks, there are larger numbers just offshore. They dive to considerable depths to take molluscs, crustaceans and small fish.

Smew   (150: good estimate)
This small sawbill occurs in only a very few regular haunts, mainly in the southern and eastern half of the country. It rarely leaves freshwater habitat, where it feeds on fish.

Red-breasted Merganser   (7,500: a provisional estimate)
Perhaps as many as 2,000 pairs breed in Britain, joined by some winter visitors from Iceland and Scandinavia. Numbers remain fairly constant, however, at counted localities from August through to April, so migrants are probably not numerous. Although breeding beside lochs and rivers well inland, the Red-breasted Merganser is a more coastal species than its relative the Goosander, and is nearly exclusively so in winter. As well as some large gatherings in the bigger

estuaries, it also occurs in small numbers scattered widely round the coasts of northern Britain. It is almost entirely a fish-eater, taking a wide variety of species, including trout and salmon, thus earning the active dislike of fishermen.

Goosander   (4,000: a provisional estimate)
The Goosander is not as numerous a breeding species as the Red-breasted Merganser, with about 1,000–1,500 pairs. Some migrants come from Scandinavia and possibly Iceland. Although the larger flocks are found in the larger firths and estuaries, some birds remain inland to winter. Its diet is very similar to that of the Red-breasted Merganser.

Oystercatcher   (200,000: a good estimate based on fairly complete counts)
The estimated number of breeding pairs in Britain is about 30,000, widely distributed over the northern half of the country, and sparingly round the coasts in the south. The population rises to a peak in September and maintains a high level until at least January. The largest wintering flocks are in excess of 40,000. The north-west European total, including Britain, is over 500,000. The typical food of the Oystercatcher are bivalves prised from rocks, but they also probe for softer items in the mud and sand.

Ringed Plover   (20,000–25,000: fairly good estimate)
The breeding population of Britain is probably about 5,500 pairs, mainly in the north of the country and around the coasts of eastern England. Peak numbers are present in our estuaries from August to October and again in May, with only about half that number during the winter months. Ringed Plovers are found on particularly sandy estuaries and on shingle stretches, where they feed on small insects, molluscs and worms.

Golden Plover   (not less than 200,000: a guess)
The number of Golden Plover found on or near wetlands in Britain is only a small proportion of the total in the country, with the majority found on inland farmland, feeding on small insects, worms and seeds. Up to 50,000 have been counted on estuaries, with maximum numbers present from November to February. The Golden Plover breeds widely in Scotland and northern England and a total of about 30,000 pairs has been suggested.

Grey Plover   (15,000: an estimate based on fairly good counts)
Not all the Grey Plover which visit our shores stay to winter, and the
peak counts are always made in September and October as passage
birds move through to countries further south. About 12,000 stay for
the winter, well spread round the country on muddy estuaries where
they probe for invertebrates.

Lapwing   (not known but some hundreds of thousands)
The Lapwing is only incidentally an estuarine or wetland bird, being
very widespread over all types of farmland. Counts at estuaries have
produced peaks of up to 150,000 in mid-winter. Their main food is
small insects in the soil, while on estuaries they take a variety of
invertebrates.

Turnstone   (10,000–12,000: a minimum estimate)
Because Turnstones are content to live in small flocks on rocky
coasts, as well as in the estuaries, a fair number may have missed
being counted by the Estuaries Enquiry. Peak counts occur in
September, indicating an onward passage, but only drop slightly to a
winter level of 9,000–11,000. The largest numbers are found in north-
west England and Scotland, though smaller flocks occur in estuaries
all round the country. Their invertebrate food is found in crevices in
rocks, and under stones.

Little Stint   (200–300: estimated)
A passage migrant in very small numbers, often only ones and twos,
though found in many estuaries, mainly in the autumn. They search
for invertebrates in the mud by rapid probing with the bill.

Purple Sandpiper   (14,000–23,000: an estimate)
The majority of Purple Sandpipers in Britain winter in small numbers
on rocky coasts where they have thus far escaped being counted.
Numbers in estuaries rarely total more than about 750, most of which
are in Scotland. They come from breeding grounds in Scandinavia
and reach a peak in November, maintaining their numbers through to
May. They feed on small animals concealed in seaweed and in rock
crevices.

Dunlin   (550,000: a fairly good estimate based on counts)
This is easily our most numerous wader, found in some very large
flocks in excess of 50,000, as well as quite tiny groups, often at inland

floods or the muddy margins of reservoirs. A few thousand pairs of Dunlin breed in Britain, but the wintering hordes come mainly from the northern USSR. Numbers build up rapidly during the late summer and the autumn months to reach a peak in October or November, departures beginning in February. The population in north-west Europe, excluding Britain, is put at about 650,000 or only very slightly larger than our total. Small invertebrates make up the bulk of the food, found by probing in the upper layers of mud and sand.

Curlew Sandpiper   (c.100: estimated)
A species which normally only comes to Britain as an uncommon autumn passage migrant. Just occasionally (the last time in 1969) several thousand may pass through, mainly on the east and south coasts. Their food and feeding habits are similar to those of the Dunlin.

Knot   (300,000–350,000: estimate based on fairly good counts)
The Knot is the second most numerous wader in Britain, after the Dunlin. It, too, occurs in very large flocks, and similarly feeds on small animals in the surface layers of the estuarine mud and sand. The peak counts in Morecombe Bay and the Ribble are of about 80,000 while other very large concentrations occur, for example in the Wash. Major arrivals occur as early as late July and numbers are maintained at a high level from October through to March or even April. Some birds are known to stay for short periods in the autumn before passing through on their way south as far as West Africa. Two separate populations are involved, coming from breeding grounds in Greenland and Canada, and from northern USSR; the former birds predominate. The peak count in Britain is slightly more than half the total in north-west Europe.

Sanderling   (25,000–30,000: estimated from counts)
Numbers of Sanderling wintering in Britain are rarely over 10,000 but there is a marked spring and autumn passage giving roughly similar peaks in May and again in July and August. In mid-winter the majority of Sanderling wintering in north-west Europe are found in Britain. The breeding grounds are in Greenland and Arctic Canada. Sanderling show a preference for sandy estuaries where they feed on insects and other small animals.

Ruff (1,000: estimated)
Small flocks of Ruff winter in a few localities in Britain, and numbers are perhaps increasing. They seek marshy areas inland as well as coastal sites, where they feed on small insects found among vegetation and in the mud. They can be found in all months of the year in scattered ones and twos.

Spotted Redshank (up to 1,000: estimated)
This is a regular passage migrant in very small numbers, often on the margins of small inland waters, pecking small insects from the water surface, and probing in the mud for other animals. Under 100 winter on our estuaries each year, mainly in the south of the country.

Redshank (90,000: a good estimate based on counts)
Between 40,000 and 50,000 pairs breed in Britain and some of these migrate south for the winter while others come in, particularly from Iceland. Substantial numbers are present on our estuaries in all months, but particularly from August through to April. In addition, small numbers, including breeding birds can be found at almost any inland water, and on wet meadows in river valleys. The British peak population represents up to three-quarters of the north-west European total. Like the other 'shanks' this species takes a wide variety of food found by probing mud, shallow water or among the stems of vegetation.

Greenshank (1,200–1,500: fair estimate)
Like its relative, the Spotted Redshank, the Greenshank is a passage migrant with peak numbers reached in late summer. Rather fewer in proportion stay for the winter. Small flocks occur in a number of southern estuaries, but perhaps as many are found in ones and twos round the margins of inland waters, large and small. Its food and feeding habits are also like those of the Spotted Redshank.

Black-tailed Godwit (5,000: good estimate based on fairly complete counts)
Black-tailed Godwits are present in Britain all the year round, with a handful of breeding pairs in several widely scattered localities, plus a few summering non-breeders. Migrants start arriving in July, building up to an August and September peak as passage through the

country takes place, then leaving a fairly steady 3,000–4,000 through the winter to March and early April. The largest numbers wintering are on the south and east coasts, though passage birds are also common further north. The north-west European population is about 40,000. Black-tailed Godwits feed by probing in deep mud but may also be found picking insects out of vegetation.

Bar-tailed Godwit   (40,000–45,000: fairly good estimate based on counts)

From breeding grounds in the USSR, Bar-tailed Godwits come to Britain for the winter, though small numbers can be found summering most years. The main arrivals are in August, with another influx in October/November, to reach peak numbers in mid-winter. Departures take place in February and March. Bar-tailed Godwits are commonest on the east coast, and in north-west England and Scotland, with rather few on the south coast and in the south-west. In the rest of north-west Europe there are about the same number as in Britain. They probe for mud-living invertebrates, the female's longer bill allowing her to feed in a slightly deeper manner than the male, thus reducing competition between the sexes.

Curlew   (not known, but probably up to 150,000)

Somewhere in excess of 50,000 pairs of Curlew breed in Britain, where they are absent only in the east and south. The winter peak is not known, but flocks on the estuaries total around 75,000. Many more Curlew feed on inland farmland and are not dependent on wetlands. Their food includes both insects of grassland and arable farmland, and worms and other small animals found by probing in mud.

Whimbrel   (2000 plus: estimate based on fairly good counts)

The Whimbrel is a passage migrant found particularly in the months of July to September, and in April and May. Occasional stragglers spend the winter, while up to 200 pairs breed in Shetland and the north of Scotland. In the main Whimbrel occur in small numbers on passage but in recent years a gathering of up to 1,000, which is quite exceptional for Britain, has been counted in late summer in Bridgwater Bay, Somerset. They probe deep in the mud for worms and other animals.

Avocet   (150–200: fairly good counts)
The Avocet breeds in small numbers in East Anglia, while small
wintering flocks are found in some south-western estuaries. They use
their unique bills to skim small insects from the very surface of the
water by side to side sweeping movements.

ENGLAND _____

AVON _____

This new county, embracing the southern part of Gloucestershire and the northern half of Somerset, contains two very important reservoirs, those of Chew and Blagdon, south of Bristol. Elsewhere inland, the county is comparatively dry, with neither the limestone of the Mendips and southern Cotswolds nor the southern part of the Severn Vale holding lakes of any size.

The coast of the Severn Estuary lying within Avon runs from Weston Bay by Weston-super-Mare to Sheperdine. Wintering flocks of waders are found at a number of localities, including Sand Bay, just north of Weston, and at Littleton and Sheperdine north of the Severn Bridge. However the single most important site is at Chittening Warth north of Avonmouth, which is one of the largest roosts in the inner estuary.

Blagdon Reservoir   Sheet 172 ST 5160

Only a couple of miles to the west of Chew Valley Lake, Blagdon is considerably smaller and not as attractive to ducks, being rather deeper and more enclosed by trees and hills. Nevertheless it still holds substantial numbers, particularly when sailing is taking place on Chew. Small lanes pass its western (dam) end, north from the village of Blagdon, and its eastern (shallow) end, north from Ubley, both villages lying on the same A368 which passes Chew. Visibility over the water is not very good, however, and in order to see the birds on the reservoir at all well one needs a permit to walk round, obtainable from Woodford Lodge beside Chew Valley Lake.

WILDFOWL

Mallard	250– 500
Teal	500–1000
Wigeon	250– 500
Shoveler	100– 250
Pochard	250– 500
Tufted Duck	250– 500

Also: Mute Swan, Gadwall, Goldeneye and Goosander
Other birds: waders on passage and terns

Chew Valley Lake (Reservoir)   *Sheet 172 ST 5760*
Lying about 11 km (7 miles) due south of Bristol, Chew Valley Lake,
as the reservoir has been named by the Water Authority, was flooded
in 1953 and covers about 490 ha (1,210 acres). It is fortunate in having
almost entirely natural banks, while a large island has greatly
enhanced its importance to breeding ducks. These include Mallard,
Shoveler, Tufted Duck, Garganey, Gadwall, Pochard, Shelduck and
Ruddy Duck. Wintering ducks are also numerous and varied, though
the introduction of sailing a few years ago has had some detrimental
effects. Fortunately the close proximity of Blagdon Reservoir (see
above) has provided a safe alternative water for the birds disturbed
from Chew on sailing days.

Chew Lake is ringed by roads; the A368 (Bath to Weston) passes
the south-east side, between Bishop Sutton and West Harptree,
while at Harptree the B3114 turns right, past the western side to
Chew Stoke. Small lanes lead from this village back to Bishop Sutton.
There are several places where the reservoir can be seen well from
these roads, particularly at Herriot's Bridge on the A368 where there
is a very attractive pool on the south side of the road, as well as
extensive reed-beds and shallows in the reservoir. A path leads from
here to a public bird-watching hide. Permits to walk round parts of
the reservoir bank are available to bird-watchers wishing to make
regular visits from Woodford Lodge, the Water Authority building
on the west side of the reservoir.

WILDFOWL

Mute Swan	<100
Mallard	500–1000
Teal	250– 500
Wigeon	500–1000
Shoveler	250– 500
Pochard	250– 500
Tufted Duck	250– 500
Goosander	<100

Also: Gadwall, Goldeneye
Other birds: passage waders, Great Crested Grebes, terns

Chittening Warth   *Sheet 172 ST 5383*
This is the name given to a small area of high saltmarsh on the banks
of the River Severn between Avonmouth and Severn Beach. It forms

a high tide roost for quite large numbers of waders which spread out
to feed over a wide area of mudflats when the water recedes.

Chittening Warth can be approached off the A403 (Avonmouth to
Aust) which runs parallel to the shore. It is necessary to find one's
way through or round the industrial complex just north of
Avonmouth, and perhaps the better way is from the north, by
walking south along the shore from Severn Beach, a village
signposted to the left off the A403.

WADERS

Ringed Plover	250– 500
Turnstone	100– 250
Dunlin	2500–5000
Redshank	100– 250
Bar-tailed Godwit	100– 250
Curlew	250– 500

Also: Grey Plover, Knot

BEDFORDSHIRE ⎯⎯⎯⎯

There are no major wetlands in Bedfordshire, but gravel and clay pits
and a number of lakes provide habitat for small numbers of the
commoner ducks, together with some Canada Geese. The best waters
are those in the valley of the Ouse, between Sandy and Wyboston.
Those at Felmersham, north-west of Bedford, are also attractive to
birds. Stewartby, a few miles south-west of Bedford, has some old
clay pits which have held over 1,000 Mallard, together with other
dabbling and diving species, but sailing now takes place on the largest
lake and the ducks are less plentiful than formerly.

BERKSHIRE _____

The present county of Berkshire has lost some of its wetlands to Oxfordshire and a substantial part of the county is unsuitable chalkland. However, in the east there are some clusters of gravel pits as well as some lakes which hold useful numbers of ducks, as well as large flocks of Canada Geese. None of the waters rate detailed treatment, but most would repay visiting. They include the gravel pits at Theale (just west of Reading) and Thatcham (just west of Newbury)—both lots lying in the Kennet valley—and the largest group at Wraysbury near Staines. The latter overlap into both Buckinghamshire and Greater London, while close by are the Datchet and Staines Reservoirs. The latter are dealt with under London.

Two other waters in Berkshire—Virginia Water near Sunningdale and Great Meadow Pond in Windsor Park—are quite good for ducks, though the former is sometimes rather disturbed. At times, Mallard, Teal, Wigeon, Tufted Duck and Pochard all reach three figures, while a speciality of the area is the Mandarin, which now lives completely feral. Up to 100 may be seen together.

BUCKINGHAMSHIRE ____

There are four wetlands in Buckinghamshire that are quite important for wildfowl although not qualifying for detailed treatment. In the south of the county, in the Thames valley, there are some good gravel pits at Marlow which attract diving ducks in some numbers, as well as small numbers of inland passage waders. There are more gravel pits just west of Newport Pagnell which have been the site of some detailed research into the ecology of such pits, and in particular their value to wildfowl, carried out by the Game Conservancy and sponsored by the owners, the Amey Roadstone Company. Part of the area has been made a reserve, and various improvements carried out to encourage both breeding and wintering ducks.

The other two waters are reservoirs; at Foxcote, just north of Buckingham, and Weston Turville near Wendover. The latter is sailed on and is too disturbed to carry more than small numbers of duck, but Foxcote is better and attracts a good variety of species, though no large flocks.

CAMBRIDGESHIRE

Although so much of the Cambridgeshire fens used to be a paradise for wildfowl, only deliberately flooded areas now remain. By swallowing up Huntingdonshire, the new county of Cambridgeshire has gained a very large reservoir, Grafham Water, to add to two areas of winter flooded land. The larger of these, the Ouse Washes, overlaps into Norfolk but will be dealt with in its entirety here. It is arguably the finest wetland in the country. The second area, the Whittlesey Washes, floods much less often than it used to but, when it does, carries large numbers of birds.

Elsewhere in Cambridgeshire there are several groups of small gravel pits which attract small numbers of typical ducks.

Grafham Water   *Sheet 153 TL 1568*

While this large 650 ha (1,600 acre) reservoir was being flooded in the mid-1960s it attracted very large numbers of ducks, especially Mallard, as well as a wide variety of freshwater waders. As soon as it was filled, however, intensive sailing and fishing started and the number of birds fell sharply. The two arms at the western end where the feeder streams enter was designated as a nature reserve but unfortunately other recreational interests have not always respected it sufficiently. The water area involved is very small in relation to the total area of the reservoir and consequently its value to birds disturbed by the sailing is small. The number of birds using the reservoir, while moderately large, is certainly well below its potential given a large area free from disturbance.

The reservoir lies a little over 1.5 km (1 mile) west of the A1 between St Neots and Huntingdon. A clearly signposted road, the B661, leads from the A1 at Buckden roundabout. This passes the dam, then runs fairly close to the south shore bringing one to the sailing club and past a number of public car parks which make excellent vantage points. From the sailing club car park it is possible to walk to a bird-watching hide overlooking the reserve area, but this is only fairly rewarding. The north side of the reservoir can be inspected from a minor road leaving the B661 before the dam and going to Grafham village.

WILDFOWL

Mute Swan	< 100
Mallard	1000–2500
Teal	250– 500
Gadwall	< 100
Wigeon	250– 500
Shoveler	< 100
Pochard	100– 250
Tufted Duck	1000–2500
Goldeneye	100– 250
Goosander	< 100

Other birds: passage waders and terns

Ouse Washes *Sheet 143 TL 3976 to TL 6003*
Lying between ruler-straight rivers about half a mile apart, the Ouse Washes extend for almost 32 km (20 miles) between Earith and Denver, near Downham Market. They form a flood relief area when more water is coming down the Bedfordshire Ouse than can be quickly got rid of through the sluices at Denver. The water is then allowed to spill out into the area between the rivers and is unable to escape because of high banks on either side. At times of peak flooding the whole area of grassland disappears under several feet of water, but more usually the floods are shallow, and constantly rising and falling, producing superb winter wildfowl habitat. The onset of the floods varies from year to year but December to March usually spans the best period.

The Wildfowl Trust, the Royal Society for the Protection of Birds and the Cambridge and Isle of Ely Naturalists' Trust have all purchased blocks of land within the Ouse Washes and these conservation bodies together form easily the largest owner of land. The power that this gives them has enabled them to ward off successive threats to drain the area or turn it into a massive reservoir.

While the latter might still attract wintering ducks, it would completely prevent the breeding birds from nesting and these are nearly as exciting as the wintering birds, with Ruff and Black-tailed Godwit both regular, and Black Tern and Little Gull occasional. In addition, significant numbers of several species of duck and other waders breed in the lush grass meadows. The Wildfowl Trust has excavated a number of ponds in front of a large glassed-in observatory so that wildfowl are attracted there early in the autumn, well before any floods appear. All three organizations have put up bird-watching hides.

The Ouse Washes carry very significant numbers of Bewick's Swan, Wigeon and Teal, often the largest flocks in the country, as well as very large numbers of other species.

1. Wildfowl Trust—Welney Refuge   *Sheet 143 TL 5594*

This lies in the northern section of the Ouse Washes, and is actually in Norfolk. The village of Welney is on the west bank of the Washes at a point where the A1101 (Littleport to Wisbech) crosses them. Note that this road is cut high winter floods and if approaching from the west it may be necessary to detour round by Downham Market. The observatory is on the east bank and approached down a small unclassified road which leaves the A1101 immediately before the bridge on the crossing to Welney. The road runs close beside the high retaining banks. There is a small car park on the right of the road, beside the warden's house. The observatory is open to Wildfowl Trust members free of charge, while non-members pay a small entrance fee. The observatory and associated hides, overlooking the permanent pools with extensive floods stretching away into the distance, provide an unrivalled spectacle of thousands of ducks and hundreds of wild swans. Not only is this stretch one of the first to flood but the presence of permanent pools and the complete lack of shooting over a very large block of land contribute to the concentration here of the bulk of birds on the Washes, at least prior to the end of the shooting season.

2. RSPB Ouse Washes Reserve   *Sheet 143 TL 4786*

The approach to this reserve is on the west bank at Welches Dam. This can be reached from either Manea or Charteris. Manea lies on the B1093, a turning off the A141 between Charteris and March. If coming in from the south, turn off the A141 in Charteris onto the

B1098. In each case follow signs to Welches Dam. There is a car park at Welches Dam from which signs direct one to the various public hides. No permit is required.

3. Earith to Sutton   *Sheet 143 TL 4179*
This, the southern end of the Washes, is the last to flood, but when it does so can be very rewarding as other washes to the north become too deep for many dabbling ducks. Another good area is outside the Washes, between Earith and Bluntisham, which floods even later. Earith lies on the A1123 (Huntingdon to Ely) road. Just after crossing the bridges over the Bedford rivers, having come from the east through the village of Earith, turn left on to the B1381 for Sutton. Stop at intervals and climb the bank on the left of the road for a view over the Washes. Turn left just before entering Sutton on a lane which crosses the Washes when not too flooded. Or continue through Sutton to Mepal to bring one to yet another road crossing.

WILDFOWL

Mute Swan	250– 500
Whooper Swan	<100
Bewick's Swan	500–1000
Mallard	2500–5000
Teal	2500–5000
Gadwall	<100
Wigeon	25000+
Pintail	1000–2500
Shoveler	500–1000
Pochard	1000–2500
Tufted Duck	250– 500

Also: Greylag, Shelduck, Goldeneye, Smew
Other birds: breeding waders and wildfowl, raptors, passage waders and terns
Bewick's Swans (55% of British total) and Wigeon (18%) are easily the largest flocks in the country; Mallard, Teal, Pintail and Pochard are all among the largest.

Whittlesey or Nene Washes   *Sheet 142 TL 3300*
The flood relief area of the River Nene is similar to, but smaller than, that of the Ouse Washes—about 19 km (12 miles) long by 1.6 km (1

mile) wide. Although regular flooding in the 1950s attracted very large numbers of wildfowl, drainage improvements in the 1960s inevitably led to a decline and a lot of the land was put under the plough. Recent wet winters have produced floods once again and the wildfowl have returned in some strength.

The area is crossed at the western end by the B1040 (Whittlesey to Thorney) road and it is possible to walk up the northern bank from here. Alternatively make for Bassenhall Farm or Eldenell, reached down unclassified roads off the A605 east of Whittlesey, and then walk along the southern bank which is better for the sun. The north and south banks are accessible from Ring's Bank at the east end of the Washes off the A141 (March to Guyhirn) road.

WILDFOWL

Bewick's Swan	100– 250
Mute Swan	100– 250
Mallard	100– 250
Teal	100– 250
Wigeon	500–1000
Pintail	250– 500
Shoveler	<100
Tufted Duck	<100
Pochard	<100

Also: Whooper Swan
Other birds: passage waders

CHESHIRE

The flat Cheshire plain contains a large number of shallow meres and lakes which vary considerably in their attractiveness to wildfowl. Most hold a few hundred of the common species, such as Mallard,

Teal, Tufted Duck and Pochard. Canada Geese are also plentiful in this area. The best of the meres is Rostherne, which is dealt with below. Of the others, Tatton Park Mere, just north of Knutsford, Doddington Pool near Nantwich, and the group of flashes—or mining subsidences—between Crewe and Sandbach, are perhaps the most rewarding to visit, and all are quite readily viewable from roads and paths.

The coast of Cheshire is restricted to a very small but extremely interesting section containing parts of the estuaries of the Dee and the Mersey. Both are shared with other counties, Clywd and Merseyside respectively. The Dee will be dealt with below, but the Mersey, although a very fine wildfowl and wader area, is omitted because access is only permitted for a handful of people and there is no possibility of the ordinary bird-watcher visiting it.

Dee Estuary   *Sheets 108, 116, 117 SJ 2577*
Lying between England and Wales, the Dee estuary is best known for the very large numbers of waders found there, and for their much-photographed roost on Hilbre Island lying near the mouth on the English side. There are actually three islands—Hilbre, Little Hilbre and Little Eye—all forming part of a bird reserve, the responsibility of the local council. It is possible to walk out to the islands at low tide, though permits (obtainable from the local District Council) are needed to land on Hilbre Island.

Elsewhere observation of the estuary is not easy, though views can be obtained on the English side from tracks and unclassified roads leading down to the shore from the A540 (Heswall to West Kirby) and, on the Welsh side, from the A548 (Connah's Quay to Prestatyn) which runs close to the shore throughout its length. The main railway line to Holyhead interferes with the view from the road itself, though it is possible to cross it at a number of points, for example, at Flint, Bagillt, Mostyn Quay and Talacre. There is a good walk to the Point of Ayr from Talacre. At the head of the estuary, near the village and steelworks of Shotton, there is an extensive area of saltings on which there are several pools. The whole area is owned by the British Steel Corporation and they issue permits (reluctantly). Titles change, but try the Public Relations Officer, Shotton Steelworks. The north end of the saltings can be seen from Little Neston, reached down a side road off the A540; turn at Windle Hill.

WILDFOWL

Shelduck	2500–5000
Mallard	1000–2500
Teal	500–1000
Wigeon	500–1000
Pintail	1000–5000
Shoveler	<100
Goldeneye	<100

Also: Pochard, Tufted Duck, Scaup, Common Scoter, Red-breasted Merganser

WADERS

Oystercatcher	10000+
Ringed Plover	1000– 2500
Grey Plover	250– 500
Lapwing	2500– 5000
Turnstone	250– 500
Purple Sandpiper	<100
Dunlin	25000+
Knot	25000+
Sanderling	5000–10000
Black-tailed Godwit	500– 1000
Bar-tailed Godwit	2500– 5000
Curlew	2500– 5000

Also: Golden Plover (250–500), Curlew Sandpiper, Spotted Redshank
Other birds: divers, grebes, skuas, shearwaters, terns, auks
The flock of Pintail is over 15% of the country's total and one of the largest in Britain. For Ringed Plover, Dunlin, Knot, Sanderling, and Bar-tailed Godwit, the Dee estuary is among the top half-dozen estuaries in the country.

Rostherne Mere   *Sheet 109 SD 7484*
Of all the Cheshire meres this is the largest and deepest. It was probably originally formed by subsidence following the dissolving of underground saltbeds. It is now up to 30 m (100 ft) deep and 153 ha (330 acres) in extent. The water is fertile and eutrophic and there is little or no submerged vegetation. There are quite extensive reedbeds. The number of Mallard it carries is particularly large for a comparatively small inland water.

The whole of the mere is a National Nature Reserve and access to it is strictly by permit only. However, the A. W. Boyd Memorial Observatory is open to the public. The mere lies close to the A556 (Northwich to Altrincham) and Junction 8 of the M56. It can be reached down unclassified roads, bearing right immediately south of the motorway and passing through the village of Rostherne.

WILDFOWL

Canada Goose	100– 250
Mallard	1000–2500
Teal	500–1000
Wigeon	<100
Pintail	<100
Shoveler	100– 250
Pochard	100– 250
Tufted Duck	<100

Also: Gadwall, Goldeneye, Goosander
Other birds: passage terns, Great Crested Grebe

CLEVELAND _____

Formerly on the borders of Yorkshire and Durham, the estuary of the Tees forms a single important wetland within the new county of Cleveland.

Teesmouth   *Sheet 93 NZ 5326*
The steady reclamation and industrialization of this estuary has, not surprisingly, caused a fall in the numbers of birds using it, but it is still quite important and well worth a visit, if only to see how wild birds can exist against a backdrop of factories and refinery chimneys.

Access has changed with each successive reclamation, but the RSPB have a reserve on Cowpen Marsh and also a bird-watching hide open to the public.

WILDFOWL

Shelduck	1000–2500
Mallard	500–1000
Teal	100– 500
Wigeon	100– 250
Pintail	<100
Shoveler	<100
Pochard	100– 250
Tufted Duck	<100

Also: Goldeneye

WADERS

Oystercatcher	250– 500
Lapwing	500– 1000
Turnstone	100– 250
Dunlin	5000–10000
Knot	5000–10000
Sanderling	250– 500
Redshank	500– 1000
Bar-tailed Godwit	250– 500

Also: Ringed Plover (100–250), Grey Plover, Golden Plover (100–250), Little Stint, Purple Sandpiper, Ruff
Other birds: diver, seaduck, terns

CORNWALL ─────────

The peninsula county of Cornwall is not particularly blessed with good wetlands. The rivers are mostly short, and where there might be estuaries the rocky nature of the coast prevents the formation of wide, flat river mouths. Two such, the estuaries of the Hayle and the Camel, both on the north coast, qualify for detailed treatment. Elsewhere there are small numbers of typical ducks and waders found in the extensive but not very rich Fal estuary between Truro and Falmouth and St. Mawes, and on the very much smaller Fowey and Gannel estuaries.

Inland waters are both scarce and unproductive, with the exception of two coastal sites; Loe Pool near Helston and Marazion Marsh, on the north side of Mount's Bay, just east of Penzance. The former is a large, shallow lake formed by the blocking of the mouth of the River Cober by a shingle bar thrown up by the sea. It can be approached down two tracks running from the B3304 (Helston to Porthleven). It lies on private land and bird-watchers are asked to keep to the tracks. Small numbers of a fair variety of duck can be found in the winter months. Marazion Marsh lies beside the A394 (Helston to Penzance), just west of the village of Marazion, and can be viewed readily from the road. It is well known as a mecca for birdwatchers on account of its strategic position at the extreme south-west of the country. Spring and autumn wader passage is particularly noteworthy and there is a long list of rarities which have occurred there.

Camel Estuary   *Sheet 200 SW 9774*

Although this estuary is about 13 km (8 miles) long, only the upper end, towards Wadebridge, is of any importance to waterfowl. Here the sand of the lower estuary gives way to a more muddy substratum in which there is a rich invertebrate life, and on which quite large areas of saltings have become established. These are particularly prominent where two small tributaries enter at Dinham and Trewarnan. Here are the best areas for birds and, fortunately, the best places for observing them. The southern side of the upper estuary is bounded by a disused railway line along which it is possible to walk for the first mile or so out of Wadebridge. It is then unfortunately cut by a creek. Further west one or two tracks lead to the river. On the north side it is possible to get close to the water at various points off the B3314 (Wadebridge to Port Isaac) road.

Also on the north side of the estuary is the small 17 ha (42 acre) Walmesley Sanctuary of the Cornwall Bird-Watching and Preservation Society. This comprises wet grassland and was created in 1939 as a protected area for waders and for the small flock of White-fronted Geese wintering on the Camel. The latter have declined in recent years, as they have elsewhere in the country, but the sanctuary is still important to them and bird-watchers are asked to keep away from the sanctuary and thus let it fulfil its vital role in providing even a small area free from disturbance.

WILDFOWL

Mute Swan	<100
White-fronted Goose	<100
Shelduck	100–250
Teal	<100
Wigeon	250–500

Also: Brent Goose, Pintail, Shoveler, Goldeneye

WADERS

Oystercatcher	250– 500
Golden Plover	2500–5000
Lapwing	2500–5000
Curlew	500–1000
Dunlin	500–1000

Also: Grey Plover, Turnstone (100–250), Knot, Sanderling, Redshank (100–250), Whimbrel
Other birds: small numbers of Red-throated Divers and Slavonian Grebes

Hayle Estuary   *Sheet 203 SW 5537*
This estuary, on the north coast between St Ives and Hayle, has two arms, of which the major, south-pointing one, running back towards St Erth, is the more important for birds. Its upper basin—about 71 ha (175 acres) of sandy flats with a fringe of salt marsh—is the principal feeding area, while the separate and non-tidal Carnsew Basin on the east bank acts as an additional and permanent roost. The main A30 (Hayle to Penzance) road follows the eastern and southern shores, giving excellent views, while the A3074, which leaves it for St Ives, runs up the west side, but further away and with a railway in between. Distances are nowhere great as the estuary is only about 0.4 km (¼ mile) wide and 0.8 km (½ mile) long. The eastern arm is even smaller, and less attractive, but the embanked waters at its head attract both waders and wildfowl. It, too, is bordered by the A30, leaving Hayle for Camborne.

WILDFOWL

Mute Swan	<100
Shelduck	<100

Teal	100– 250
Wigeon	500–1000

Also: Goldeneye, Red-breasted Merganser and Goosander

WADERS

Golden Plover	250– 500
Lapwing	500–1000
Dunlin	250– 500

Also: Oystercatcher, Ringed Plover (100–250), Turnstone, Knot, Sanderling, Redshank, Bar-tailed Godwit, Curlew
Other birds: Slavonian Grebe (in Carnsew Basin)

CUMBRIA

Cumbria is bounded north and south by two great estuaries, the Solway Firth and Morecambe Bay. In between comes the Lake District with high fells and deep, mainly oligotrophic, lakes of small value to wildfowl. Elsewhere the coast is of little interest apart from the Duddon estuary, just across the Furness peninsula from Morecambe Bay.

Morecambe Bay lies partly in Lancashire and is detailed under that county. The Solway Firth, the border between England and Scotland, is also shared, but as access to both sides of it is not easy within a short space of time, the southern shore will be dealt with here, the northern shore under Dumfries and Galloway.

Duddon Estuary   *Sheet 96 SD 2078*
Like Morecambe Bay, the Duddon estuary is more noted for its waders than its wildfowl, which seem to find little to their liking on the principally sandy flats. The total area is some 3,800 ha (9,400 acres) including about 400 ha (990 acres) of saltmarsh. Waders are quite plentiful, though few in comparison with the wealth of Morecambe Bay next door. However observation possibilities are relatively good. Sanderling and Redshank are present in particularly high numbers.

A railway line runs right round the estuary with the main roads, the A595 and A5093, outside it. Starting in the south-east corner at Askam on the A595, roads lead to the left down to the shore at Marsh Grange, a mile and a half north of Askam, and again at Soutergate. A footpath along the shore connects the two places. Further round, near the head of the estuary at Broughton, unclassified roads lead to Foxfield and a track crosses a level crossing near the station and so down to the shore. On the west bank there is access down unclassified roads or tracks at The Green (make for Green Road Station and then over the line to the shore) and at Millom (again crossing the line by the station and then turning left). A footpath running along the back of the saltings connects these two access points. If, instead of turning left behind Millom station, one goes straight on, the road leads to the coast north of Hodbarrow Point to which a coastal footpath runs.

WILDFOWL: rather little information but a few hundred each of Shelduck, Mallard, Teal, Wigeon and Pintail.

WADERS

Oystercatcher	5000–10000
Ringed Plover	250– 500
Lapwing	500– 1000
Turnstone	100– 250
Dunlin	5000–10000
Knot	1000– 2500
Sanderling	1000– 2500
Redshank	1000– 2500
Curlew	1000– 2500

Also: Bar-tailed Godwit (100–250)
Other birds: a resident flock of Greylag Geese

South Solway   *Sheet 85 NY 1456 to NY 3462*
There are two distinct areas on the south side of the Solway Firth: Moricambe Bay just north of Silloth (NY 1757), and the inner firth from Port Carlisle to Rockcliffe (NY 3060). Moricambe Bay is a broad estuary fed by two rivers, the Waver and the Wampool. Duck numbers are not known with any accuracy but include some hundreds of Wigeon and Mallard as well as Teal, Pintail, Shoveler and Shelduck. Good numbers of waders occur, though they are not easy to see except at high tide.

Access is either from Silloth on the south side, from where take an unclassified road to Skinburness then walk out to Grune Point, or, on the north side, an unclassified road leaves Kirkbride from the B5307 (Carlisle to Silloth) heading for Cardurnock. On its way it skirts the River Wampool, giving good views over the estuary, except that one is looking into the sun rather, especially near Anthorn.

Continuing on this road through Cardurnock, Bowness and Port Carlisle brings one in sight of the inner estuary, particularly from the Port Carlisle to Drumburgh road. However the channel of the River Eden is usually on this side of the estuary, preventing close views. Turning left in Burgh-by-Sands brings one to a sign indicating the monument to Edward I. A footpath leads down to the monument and beyond, on the east edge of Burgh Marsh.

Like Moricambe Bay, this marsh is fairly heavily shot but it nevertheless carries regular flocks of Pink-footed and sometimes Barnacle Geese as well as flocks of ducks and waders. There are also views from here over Rockcliffe Merse. Rockcliffe is very important for wintering waders and geese and to breeding birds. Although it is possible to get permission to walk over the Merse—though not during the breeding season—the enormous area of completely flat saltmarsh without any cover means that it is almost impossible to get close to the birds without disturbing them badly, and it is one of those areas best left undisturbed.

WILDFOWL (*spring peaks*)

Pink-footed Goose	5000–10000
Barnacle Goose	5000–10000

WADERS

Oystercatcher	10000–25000
Ringed Plover	1000– 2500
Golden Plover	5000–10000
Grey Plover	100– 250
Lapwing	10000–25000
Turnstone	250– 500
Dunlin	5000–10000
Sanderling	250– 500
Knot	10000–25000
Redshank	2500– 5000
Greenshank	<100

Black-tailed Godwit	100– 250
Bar-tailed Godwit	2500– 5000
Curlew	5000–10000

Also: Spotted Redshank, Whimbrel.
Oystercatcher (10% of British total), Ringed Plover (10%), Redshank (5%), and Bar-tailed Godwit (13%) emphasize the importance of the South Solway for waders. The Golden Plover and Lapwing numbers are among the highest estuarine flocks.

DERBYSHIRE

This county stretches from the High Peak area between Manchester and Sheffield, containing comparatively sterile hill reservoirs such as the Derwent and Ladybower, south to the Trent valley. In the southern part of the county there are a number of park lakes, as at Kedleston, Osmaston, Locko and Allestree. Each holds small numbers of ducks, together with flocks of Canada Geese, especially at Kedleston. Two reservoirs are rather more attractive: at Ogston, near Matlock, and at Staunton Harold, on the Leicestershire border, north-east of Swadlincote.

DEVON

Like neighbouring Cornwall, much of the Devon coast is cliff-girt and inhospitable to waterfowl, but the rivers are longer and larger, and the cliffs relent to allow the formation of a number of quite extensive, complex estuaries rich in birdlife. Four of these—the Tamar, Kingsbridge and Exe estuaries on the south coast, and the combined estuary of the Taw and Torridge rivers on the north coast—receive full treatment below. Other minor estuaries include the Yealm, Erme, Avon, Dart, Otter and Axe. All hold small numbers of the commoner ducks and waders. Inland Devon has negligible numbers of wildfowl. Moorland reservoirs are too bleak and infertile and park lakes mostly too small. Only Tamar Lake, a reservoir in the headwaters of the Tamar River, above Bude, seems attractive, holding flocks of a hundred or more Mallard, Teal, Pochard and Tufted Duck.

Exe Estuary   *Sheet 192 SX 9884*

The estuary of the river Exe is by far the most important wetland of south-west England. It is also very large, about 8 km × 1.5 km (5 miles × 1 mile) though not all of it is of equal importance for birds. There are about 820 ha (2,000 acres) of mudflats in all, together with nearly 240 ha (600 acres) of marsh, mostly near the head at Exminster. The flats comprise sand and mud, and on the latter there are considerable growths of *Zostera* and *Enteromorpha* providing food for the very large flocks of Wigeon and the increasing numbers of Brent Geese. They are concentrated in the lower half of the estuary.

The estuary can be viewed from a number of points on either shore, though the west side is better as much of it is a sanctuary which the birds make full use of, while the east side is more built up, especially round Exmouth. The village of Lympstone, off the A377 (Exeter to Exmouth), gives perhaps the best views on the east side, with a public footpath running south from here alongside the railway line. The mouth of the estuary can be seen well from Exmouth promenade.

On the west side, the A379 (Exeter to Dawlish) goes past Powderham where it is possible to cross the intervening railway line on a level crossing and so gain access to the seawall. From there a public footpath runs north up the bank of the estuary. Further south, at Powderham Park, stop where the River Kenn passes under the coastal road. Finally, leave the main road for Dawlish Warren, where there is a car park, and from there one can walk over the dunes which give views both out over the sea and into the estuary. This last place can be particularly rewarding.

WILDFOWL

Mute Swan	<100
Brent Goose	500–1000
Shelduck	250– 500
Mallard	500–1000
Teal	250– 500

Wigeon	2500–5000
Pintail	<100
Goldeneye	<100
Eider	<100
Red-breasted	
Merganser	<100

Also: Canada Goose (100–250), Shoveler, Pochard, Tufted Duck, Scaup, Common Scoter

The flock of Brent Geese, all Dark-bellied, has increased considerably in recent years in line with national trends.

WADERS

Oystercatcher	2500– 5000
Ringed Plover	250– 500
Golden Plover	250– 500
Grey Plover	250– 500
Turnstone	250– 500
Dunlin	5000–10000
Knot	250– 500
Sanderling	100– 250
Redshank	500– 1000
Black-tailed Godwit	500– 1000
Bar-tailed Godwit	500– 1000
Curlew	500– 1000

Also: Lapwing (500–1,000), Purple Sandpiper, Curlew Sandpiper, Ruff, Spotted Redshank, Greenshank, Whimbrel, Avocet
Other birds: grebes, passage terns and skuas

Kingsbridge Estuary   *Sheet 202 SX 7441*

The upper part of this estuary is best for birds, where there is an extensive area of sand and mudflats divided into the two main arms of the Kingsbridge estuary proper and Frogmore Creek. Both can be seen, particularly the former, from the A379 (Kingsbridge to Dartmouth) on either side of the village of West Charleton. Other views can only be obtained by walking, and on the west bank this is even more necessary. A public footpath runs along the north bank of Frogmore Creek, starting in Frogmore village.

WILDFOWL

Mute Swan	<100
Shelduck	100– 500
Wigeon	500–1000
Goldeneye	<100
Red-breasted	
Merganser	<100

Also: Mallard, Teal, Shoveler, Tufted Duck, Scaup

WADERS

Oystercatcher	250– 500
Golden Plover	500–1000
Lapwing	500–1000
Dunlin	500–1000
Redshank	250– 500
Curlew	250– 500

Also: Ringed Plover, Grey Plover, Turnstone, Knot, Greenshank

Tamar Estuary   *Sheet 201 SX 4359*

There are four main parts to the Tamar estuary: two western arms—the Lynher estuary and St John's Lake; and two northern arms—those of the rivers Tamar and Tavy. To what extent they are interdependent is unclear, but each can provide rewarding bird-watching. The more important pair is Lynher and St John's Lake which between them have about 570 ha (1,400 acres) of rich mudflats and saltmarsh.

The Lynher estuary can be seen very well from the A374 which runs along the south side westwards from Torpoint. The best place is just west of the village of Anthony. St John's Lake may be watched from the south end of Torpoint itself, or its head from the village of St John. The Tamar and Tavy estuaries are also quite accessible, with roads leading to small villages along the shore. Horsham and Bere Ferrers are the best places from which to cover the Tavy, while Weirquay on the east bank and Cargreen on the west bank provide good observation of the Tamar. Cargreen is the best locality for seeing the wintering flock of Avocets. Any of these villages can be approached from Plymouth, Tavistock or via Saltash, but the area contains a maze of lanes and careful attention to a map is necessary.

WILDFOWL

Mute Swan	<100
Shelduck	250– 500
Mallard	250– 500
Teal	100– 500
Wigeon	2500–5000

Also: Pintail, Scaup, Goldeneye, Red-breasted Merganser

WADERS

Oystercatcher	250– 500
Golden Plover	1000–2500
Lapwing	500–1000
Dunlin	2500–5000
Knot	500–1000
Redshank	1000–2500
Black-tailed Godwit	250– 500
Curlew	500–1000
Avocet	100– 250

Also: Ringed Plover, Grey Plover, Turnstone (100–250), Spotted Redshank, Greenshank and Bar-tailed Godwit

Taw-Torridge Estuary   *Sheet 180 SS 4732*

Two estuaries—the Taw running about 13 km (8 miles) west from Barnstaple, and the shorter, narrower Torridge, stretching 6.5 km (4 miles) north from Bideford—meet in a broad basin protected from the sea by the massive dune systems of Braunton Burrows on the north side and Northam Burrows on the south. Wildfowl and wader numbers are moderate but of good variety. Braunton Burrows provides the better vantage point but with the disadvantage of looking into the light. Access here is restricted at times by military activity, so look out for red flags. When there are no restrictions— and our forces mostly seem to work a five-day week—it is possible to walk right out to Crow Point at the tip of the Burrows, the starting point being the town of Braunton which lies on the A361 (Barnstaple to Ilfracombe). Turn left just before entering Braunton, then left over a level-crossing on to a lane beside the river Caen. A public footpath then runs along the seawall to the point. Northam Burrows are accessible from Appledore or Northam, north of Bideford. Public footpaths run along the seawall from Instow, on the east bank of the Torridge, north and east to the junction with the Taw.

WILDFOWL

Mute Swan	<100
Shelduck	100–250
Mallard	100–250
Teal	100–250
Wigeon	250–500

Also: Brent Goose, Pochard, Goldeneye, Eider

WADERS

Oystercatcher	1000– 2500
Ringed Plover	250– 500
Golden Plover	2500– 5000
Grey Plover	<100
Lapwing	5000–10000
Turnstone	100– 250
Dunlin	2500– 5000
Knot	100– 250
Sanderling	100– 250
Redshank	500– 1000
Curlew	1000– 2500

Also: Ruff, Black-tailed Godwit, Bar-tailed Godwit, Greenshank, Whimbrel
Other birds: seabirds off the points

DORSET

This undulating county is mainly founded on chalk and therefore lacks any extensive inland water. On the coast there are three notable wetlands—The Fleet, Radipole Lake and Poole Harbour—which are all dealt with below. Lodmoor, a reed-grown marsh just east of Weymouth on the coast road, is still excellent for breeding birds, but the absence of much open water prevents large numbers of duck from wintering. However, migrant waders find it attractive. Another quite good site is Portland Harbour, skirted by the A354 running out to Portland Bill. Here small numbers of divers, grebes and seaducks can be found in winter. The last include Eiders and Scoters and up to 200 Red-breasted Mergansers.

The River Frome, making its way through its broad, flat valley between Dorchester and Wareham, not infrequently floods in winter and flocks of ducks and, recently, Bewick's Swans, are attracted to the wet meadows, particularly in the area a few miles to the east of Dorchester.

The Fleet   *Sheet 194 SY 6082*

The extraordinary geological formation of Chesil Beach, a great shingle bank stretching about 29 km (18 miles) from West Bay to Portland Bill, encloses within its eastern half The Fleet, a shallow, brackish, tidal lagoon, varying in width between 230 m (250 yards), and about 1,200 m (¾ mile). There is a single narrow opening to the sea at the extreme eastern end where the outlet runs under the road at Ferrybridge into Portland Harbour. Within The Fleet are the largest beds of *Zostera* (all three species occurring together) in the country, together with extensive areas of *Ruppia*. These provide food for the large numbers of wintering Wigeon as well as for Mute Swans. The latter breed colonially at the western end of The Fleet in the famous Abbotsbury Swannery, where they have been protected for centuries. The Swannery is open to the public between the beginning of May and the middle of September and is signposted from Abbotsbury village, which lies on the B3157 (Weymouth to Bridport) road.

Small tracks and unclassified lanes also lead off this road and give access to a signposted public footpath which runs along much of the northern bank of The Fleet. This gives very good views of the two large bays of East Fleet and Langton Herring (where the footpath turns inland) where most of the wintering duck will be found. There is no footpath round the Swannery bay, nor along the Chesil Beach which is also strictly wardened in the summer to protect breeding terns. A small number of waders are found on the beaches of the large bays of The Fleet, and also at the eastern end by Ferrybridge. Like Portland Harbour, this latter area is visible from the A354 (Weymouth to Portland) where there is a convenient large car park.

WILDFOWL

The number of pairs of Mute Swans breeding in the colony at Abbotsbury varies between about 30 and 50, while the total number of swans on The Fleet moves between a summer low of around 400 to a winter peak of 800–900. The Wigeon population is third in importance to the Exe and Tamar estuaries in south-west England.

Mute Swan	500–1000
Wigeon	2500–5000
Pintail	<100
Shoveler	<100
Pochard	100– 250
Tufted Duck	<100
Goldeneye	<100

Also: Brent Goose (100–250), Shelduck, Mallard (100–250), Teal (100–250), Gadwall, Red-breasted Merganser

WADERS: Oystercatcher, Ringed Plover, Grey Plover, Lapwing (500–1,000), Dunlin (250–500), Redshank, Bar-tailed Godwit
Other birds: Common and Little Terns breed on Chesil Beach. Several thousand Coot winter on The Fleet.

Poole Harbour *Sheet 194 SY/SZ 0090*

The total extent of this shallow and complex indentation is about 2,200 ha (5,400 acres), about half each of mudflats—mostly comprised of clay and silt—and *Spartina* and *Phragmites* marshes. Neither the mudflats nor the marshes are particularly rich in food, and this, combined with the fairly extensive disturbance from public recreation, reduces the number of wildfowl able to live here. Brownsea Island, out in the harbour, with its two freshwater pools, provides safe roosting for the ducks. There are several vantage points along the shore road between Poole and the Sandbanks Ferry but on the south side virtually the only easy place to reach is the road between the Ferry and Studland. On the east side of this is the Studland Heath National Nature Reserve, with its own hide overlooking Little Sea, a favoured bird spot. Note that Poole Harbour experiences a very irregular tidal pattern.

WILDFOWL

Mute Swan	<100
Shelduck	1000–2500
Mallard	500–1000
Teal	500–1000
Wigeon	500–1000
Tufted Duck	250– 500
Goldeneye	<100
Red-breasted Merganser	100– 250

Also: Canada Goose (250–500), Brent Goose (100–250), Shoveler, Pochard (100–250), Scaup (100–250), Eider

WADERS

Oystercatcher	500–1000
Ringed Plover	100– 250
Dunlin	1000–2500
Redshank	500–1000
Black-tailed Godwit	250– 500
Bar-tailed Godwit	<100

Also: Grey Plover, Turnstone, Lapwing (250–500)
Other birds: divers, grebes, terns

Radipole Lake, Weymouth   *Sheet 194 SY 6780*

The lake was formed by the blocking off of the estuary of the River Wey. The outer part is now Weymouth harbour and yacht basin, while the inner part extends from a concrete-rimmed area bounded by a fun-fair and an enormous car park back into an increasingly more natural area of reedbeds, muddy shallows and open water. The RSPB recently declared a reserve over the greater part of the natural area of reeds and lake. Access to the edges of the lake is direct from the town centre, while public paths traverse some of the reed marsh. A road along the east bank gives excellent views of the open north end of the lake where many of the duck congregate.

WILDFOWL
Up to 20 pairs of Mute Swans breed in the reeds; peak numbers are in the summer months.

Mute Swan	100–250
Mallard	100–250
Teal	100–250
Shoveler	<100
Pochard	250–500
Tufted Duck	250–500

Waders: Low-water level reveals an attractive mud area visible from the car park on the south-east corner of the lake, and brings in a wide variety of passage migrants.

Other birds: Bearded Tits and warblers breed in the reeds. Passage terns and gulls, especially Little Gull, are quite plentiful.

CO. DURHAM

Since county boundary reorganization, Durham has lost Tees estuary, its sole coastal wetland, and also Scaling Dam above Loftus. Both now lie in Cleveland, where the former is described in detail. Durham is left with a number of inland, mainly high ground, reservoirs whose value to wildfowl is small.

ESSEX

The combination of several large shallow estuaries, coastal saltings and mudflats, and two large drinking water reservoirs makes Essex one of the most important wildfowl and wader areas in the country. It is the first landfall for many species coming from the east in the autumn and so is equally important as a migration area as it is for its great wintering flocks.

Progressing round the immensely long coastline, starting in the Thames estuary, the first ducks are met with in the area of East Tilbury where Pintail and Mallard occur in some hundreds, while small numbers of waders, including Dunlin and Redshank, occur on the saltings. Further down the estuary there is little exposed mud and much industry until the east end of Canvey Island is reached. Here are the Leigh marshes, the first flock of Dark-bellied Brent Geese—which are more numerous in Essex than any other county—and considerable flocks of waders. Round the corner past Southend are the great mudflats of Maplin Sands, off Foulness Island, a vitally important site for Brent Geese and other waterfowl. Next comes the Crouch estuary—mostly rather narrow except near Fambridge where the river broadens round a marshy island—once reclaimed but now largely returned to the sea. North of the Crouch is the broad area of mudflat and saltings of the Dengie peninsula, taking one to the great estuary of the River Blackwater, stretching many miles inland to Maldon. On the north side, near the mouth, it is joined by the estuary of the Crouch. North again—past the holiday resorts of Clacton and Frinton, and nearly enclosed by arms of land—is Hamford Water where mud, saltings and islands are intricately mixed. Finally, and forming the border with Suffolk, is the Stour estuary.

Inland waters in Essex consist mainly of small ponds and private lakes, of which there are many, with the notable exceptions of Abberton and Hanningfield reservoirs. The first is one of the best such waters in the country for ducks. The newer Ardleigh reservoir north of Colchester is heavily used for recreation and holds only moderate numbers of the common species.

Abberton Reservoir   *Sheet 168 TL 9718*

Essex is blessed not just with magnificent coastal wetlands but also with one of the finest reservoirs for wildfowl in the country. It gains immeasurably from being only a short distance from the coast, and so acts as a haven for many estuarine birds which appreciate the sanctuary from shooting that it provides. A bird-ringing station has been established at the reservoir for nearly 30 years and many thousands of birds, particularly ducks, are caught and ringed each year providing much valuable information.

Abberton Reservoir lies midway between Colchester and the Blackwater estuary, about 7 km (4 miles) from each. Completed in 1940, its total water surface is about 500 ha (1,240 acres), and is divided into three sections. The largest, and lowest, is completely embanked with concrete but this does not prevent it holding extremely large numbers of ducks, both roosting and feeding. The upper two sections have natural banks and so attract a wider variety of birds. Drawdown can lead to extensive mudbanks which bring in feeding waders.

Access within the perimeter fence is restricted to a small number of permit holders, all members of the Essex Bird Watching and Preservation Society. However, much can be seen from the two causeways crossing the reservoir, and from a public bird-watching hide. The B1026 (Colchester to Maldon) crosses the reservoir between the main and middle sections. On the main section side, at the north end of the causeway, there is an enclosure containing a small collection of European wildfowl, together with a public hide overlooking a wide bay in which artificial islands have been placed to attract breeding terns and other birds.

A short distance before reaching the causeway, coming from the north, there is a gateway on the left from which good views can be obtained over one of the large bays of the main section. A little further on, past the causeway, there are views over another of the bays, from the road. Continuing on the B1026 for about a mile, and where the road takes a sharp left-hand bend, turn right on to an unclassified road for Layer Breton. This road crosses back over the reservoir on a causeway between the upper and middle sections, both of which have natural banks and a certain amount of emergent vegetation.

Although primarily a winter haunt of ducks, there are often large flocks present in summer too, with up to 3,000 moulting Pochard present in recent years. Small numbers of a variety of species breed.

WILDFOWL

Mute Swan	<100
Bewick's Swan	<100
Mallard	2500–5000
Teal	500–1000
Gadwall	100– 250
Wigeon	2500–5000
Pintail	100– 250
Shoveler	250– 500
Pochard	500–1000
Tufted Duck	1000–2500
Goldeneye	250–500
Goosander	<100

Also: Canada Goose, Shelduck, Smew

Other birds: passage waders, divers, grebes and terns
The numbers of Mallard, Shoveler, Pochard, Tufted Duck and
Goldeneye are among the highest in Britain.

Blackwater Estuary   *Sheet 168 TL 8606 to TM 0010*
The Blackwater is one of the most important estuaries on the east
coast of England. The flats are composed of fine silts and sand rich in
invertebrates, and in the more muddy upper bays there are good
growths of *Zostera* and *Enteromorpha*. Mussel beds provide feeding for
small numbers of seaducks. There are considerable areas of saltmarsh,
especially on the north side, and breeding birds are quite plentiful and
varied.

There are several key areas within the whole estuary and these are
dealt with individually below, together with the numbers of
wildfowl found at each. The wader counts have been consolidated for
the whole estuary and are given here.

WADERS

Oystercatcher	500–1000
Ringed Plover	500–1000
Golden Plover	500–1000
Grey Plover	500–1000
Lapwing	1000–2500
Dunlin	10000+
Knot	500–1000
Redshank	2500–5000
Bar-tailed Godwit	100– 250
Whimbrel	<100

Also: Spotted Redshank (100–250), Greenshank (100–250), Black-tailed
Godwit

1. Mundon   *TL 9005*
Mundon lies on the B1018 (Maldon to Latchingdon) road. Turn left
towards the coast and walk to the seawall. Brent Geese and ducks are
more numerous here than elsewhere on the south side of the estuary.

WILDFOWL

Brent Goose	1000–2500
Shelduck	500–1000

Mallard	<100
Teal	100– 250
Wigeon	500–1000
Pintail	<100
Goldeneye	<100

Also: Red-breasted Merganser

2. Steeple *TL 9205*

Going east from Mundon one comes to Steeple Creek with a broad stretch of tidal mud and sand at its mouth. This sheltered area is particularly good for creek-loving waders and for Brent Geese which come close inshore here. Access is via the village of Steeple on the unclassified Latchingdon to Bradwell road. Turn left here for Stansgate Abbey Farm and then walk from this track to the seawall.

WILDFOWL

Brent Goose	250–500
Shelduck	100–250
Mallard	<100
Teal	100–250
Wigeon	100–250

Also: Shoveler, Goldeneye, Red-breasted Merganser

3. St Lawrence *TL 9606*

The area furthest east along the south side of the Blackwater, this includes a wide bay stretching eastwards to Bradwell-on-Sea. The village of St Lawrence lies on the same unclassified road from Latchingdon to Bradwell. Turn left here for Ramsey Island which lies on the seawall and then walk east.

WILDFOWL

Brent Goose	500–1000
Shelduck	100– 250
Mallard	100– 250
Wigeon	100– 250
Goldeneye	<100

Also: Red-breasted Merganser

4. North shore of Blackwater *TL 9208*

The north shore is the most important part of the estuary for both wildfowl and waders. A broad belt of mudflats reaches from the river wall out to Osea Island and, to the east, more than two-thirds of the way across the river. The shoreline is cut by tidal creeks and fringed with saltmarsh. Further east two large creeks run back towards Tollesbury and Salcott.

There are several points of access to the river wall which provides good, slightly elevated walking. All of these are from the B1026 (Maldon to Colchester). From Maldon, the first point is at Heybridge Basin, which gives views over the arm of the river running north of Northey Island. Next comes Goldhanger, a village off the A1026. Turn right in the village on to a lane which leads to the seawall. In Tolleshunt D'Arcy turn right on to the A1023 which leads to Tollesbury. Tracks lead out of the far end of the village: to the right and thence to an old railway line which can be followed to the seawall, and to the left towards the Old Hall Marshes. Turn right off this latter track for the seawall. In all areas a public footpath runs along the seawall.

WILDFOWL

Brent Goose	2500–5000
Shelduck	1000–2500
Mallard	500–1000
Teal	250– 500
Wigeon	1000–2500
Pintail	100– 250
Pochard	100– 250
Tufted Duck	<100
Goldeneye	100– 250
Eider	<100
Red-breasted Merganser	<100

Also: Mute Swan (100–250), Shoveler

Colne Estuary   *Sheet 168 TM 0617*

The River Colne runs through Colchester, remaining fairly narrow, with limited mudflats, until near its mouth it receives the wide creeks from the back of Mersea Island and from Brightlingsea. Here broader expanses of mud occur and the birds become more plentiful.

Access is not possible on the west bank because of military areas. Good views can be obtained, however, from the east point of Mersea

Island. Drive on to the island on the B1025 from Colchester and then take the first turning right. Follow this to the end and walk to the seawall.

On the other side of the Colne go to Brightingsea on the A1027 and A1029 from Colchester. Make for the Quay and then walk westwards. Further south, Colne Point and the St Osyth Marshes, a reserve of the Essex Naturalists' Trust, provide good opportunities for bird-watching.

WILDFOWL

Mute Swan	<100
Brent Goose	500–1000
Shelduck	500–1000
Mallard	500–1000
Teal	100– 500
Pochard	100– 250
Goldeneye	100– 250
Eider	<100

Also: Wigeon (250–500), Shoveler, Tufted Duck, Red-breasted Merganser

WADERS

Oystercatcher	250– 500
Ringed Plover	250– 500
Golden Plover	250– 500
Grey Plover	100– 250
Turnstone	100– 250
Lapwing	500–1000
Dunlin	5000+
Knot	<100
Sanderling	100– 250
Redshank	1000–2500
Spotted Redshank	<100
Greenshank	<100
Curlew	1000–2500

Also: Curlew Sandpiper, Black-tailed Godwit, Bar-tailed Godwit, Whimbrel

Dengie Peninsula   *Sheet 168 TM 0304*
This is one of the least accessible stretches of the Essex coast with no

roads within two or three miles of the seawall and very few farm tracks. The numbers and variety of both wildfowl and waders are important and the area is well worth the effort of a visit. It can in fact be reached from either the north or south end, but to see more than a small portion of the area it is necessary to walk several miles.

At the north end, access is via Bradwell-on-Sea, at the mouth of the Blackwater estuary. Follow the road and then the farm track to St Peter's Chapel, which lies beside the seawall. From here walk south along the top of the seawall. At the south end access is via Burnham-on-Crouch. A road heads eastwards to East Wick just before one reaches the town on the B1021 from Southminster. Following this to its end, through some farms, brings one within sight of the seawall at Holliwell Point, the southern end of the peninsula.

WILDFOWL

Brent Goose	1000–2500
Shelduck	250– 500
Mallard	1000–2500
Teal	250– 500
Wigeon	1000–2500
Pintail	100– 250

Also: Shoveler, Eider (100–250), Common Scoter, Red-breasted Merganser

WADERS

Oystercatcher	1000–5000
Ringed Plover	100– 500
Grey Plover	500–1000
Lapwing	500–1000
Turnstone	500–1000
Dunlin	5000+
Knot	2500–5000
Sanderling	100– 250
Redshank	500–1000
Curlew	1000–2500
Bar-tailed Godwit	250– 500

Also: Golden Plover (500–1,000), Spotted Redshank (100–250), Whimbrel
Other birds: raptors, Short-eared Owl

Foulness and Maplin Sands   *Sheet 178 TQ/TR 0090*
For the sake of comprehensiveness it is necessary to include this
locality even though access for all but serious bird-watchers,
carrying out census work, for example, is all but impossible. The
entire area is policed by the Ministry of Defence and permits to enter
are not readily given.

This area made the headlines a few years ago as the first choice for
London's third airport. Its vital importance to the Dark-bellied Brent
Goose population probably did not affect the final decision to cancel
the proposed airport, but at least it led to money being found for
much-needed research on the bird and its habitat. Roughly one-sixth
of the world population of this subspecies can be found here in the
early part of the winter.

There are about 12,100 ha (30,000 acres) of sand flats and
saltmarshs, making it one of the three largest continuous flats in the
country. The *Zostera noltii* which forms the principal food for the
Brent Geese covers approximately 325 ha (800 acres), also one of the
country's largest areas for this plant. Just off Foulness Point lies a
shell beach which holds a large Little Tern colony, together with
rather more pairs of Common Tern. It also forms a high-tide roost for
waders feeding both north and south of the Crouch estuary.

WILDFOWL

Brent Goose	5000–10000
Shelduck	250– 500
Mallard	250– 500
Teal	100– 250
Wigeon	1000– 2500

Also: Mute Swan (100–250), Pintail, Shoveler, Pochard (100–250), Tufted
Duck, Eider, Red-breasted Merganser. There are scattered records of
Common Scoter which suggest that quite large flocks may winter
offshore.

WADERS

Oystercatcher	5000+
Ringed Plover	250– 500
Golden Plover	500–1000
Grey Plover	250– 500
Lapwing	500–1000
Turnstone	100– 250

Dunlin	5000–10000
Knot	5000–10000
Sanderling	100– 250
Redshank	2500– 5000
Bar-tailed Godwit	1000– 2500
Curlew	2500– 5000

Also: Spotted Redshank, Greenshank, Black-tailed Godwit, Whimbrel

Hamford Water   *Sheet 169 TM 2225*

Lying between Walton-on-Naze and Harwich, Hamford Water is an intricate tangle of creeks, mudflats, saltmarsh and islands, some reclaimed, others not. The military operate on Bridgemarsh Island in the north, while the largest, Horsey Island, is private property and only accessible at low tide over a narrow causeway. Wildfowl and waders are present in large numbers during the migration periods and in winter, while breeding birds include a large Black-headed Gull colony, Common and Little Terns, Ringed Plover and Oystercatcher. The total area is about 2,200 ha (5,400 acres) of which about half is low and high level saltmarsh. *Zostera* and *Enteromorpha* are both plentiful, accounting for the large flocks of wintering Brent Geese.

It is very difficult to obtain good views of much of the area. Perhaps the best vantage point is on the east side, approaching through Walton-on-Naze. Walton can be reached from the A133 (Colchester to Clacton), turning on to the B1033 at Weeley. Keep through the town, heading north for The Naze. From the cliff top here one can walk northwards to Stone Point, though this involves crossing tidal creeks which fill at high tide. Alternatively bear west at the first creek to Walton Channel and view from here across to Horsey Island.

On the south side of Hamford Water one can look out over the broadest extent of mudflats and water from the end of the Horsey Island access causeway. This is a track heading off the B1034 at Kirby-le-Soken. It is possible to walk in either direction along the seawall from here. Access to the north side is probably not worth trying.

WILDFOWL

Brent Goose	1000–2500
Shelduck	500–1000

Mallard	100– 250
Teal	250– 500
Wigeon	250– 500
Pintail	100– 250
Red-breasted Merganser	<100

Also: Mute Swan, Shoveler, Pochard (100–250), Goldeneye, Common Scoter, Long-tailed Duck

WADERS

Ringed Plover	500–1000
Golden Plover	1000–2500
Grey Plover	500–1000
Lapwing	1000–2500
Turnstone	100– 250
Dunlin	10000+
Knot	100– 250
Sanderling	100– 250
Redshank	1000–2500
Black-tailed Godwit	100– 250
Bar-tailed Godwit	100– 250
Curlew	1000–2500

Also: Oystercatcher (250–500), Purple Sandpiper, Ruff, Spotted Red-shank, Greenshank, Whimbrel
Other birds: terns, skuas, Snow Bunting

Hanningfield Reservoir   *Sheet 167 TQ 7398*

This reservoir was constructed in 1954 and has a water area of 350 ha (870 acres). Most of it has natural banks and drawdown produces muddy areas attractive to waders as well as wildfowl. Terns, divers and grebes all occur regularly.

Access is by permit only, as at Abberton, and again those permits are held by the Essex Bird Watching Society. However, there is no need to enter the reservoir fence to see the birds as there are good vantage points at a number of places from the roads. The reservoir is more disturbed than Abberton, because of fishing, but this rarely drives all the birds away.

It is possible to drive right round the reservoir on a network of lanes, obtaining views as one goes. The two nearest classified roads are the A130 (Chelmsford to Southend) and the B1007 (Chelmsford to Billericay). Taking either of these south from Chelmsford, take the road signposted West Hanningfield, after about 10 km (6 miles). From the centre of the village take the turning for South Hanningfield and the first views of the reservoir, from near the dam, are obtained. Keep bearing to the right at each road junction and see the reservoir on your right at intervals.

WILDFOWL

Mallard	500–1000
Teal	250– 500
Gadwall	<100
Wigeon	250– 500
Pintail	<100
Shoveler	100– 250
Pochard	100– 250
Tufted Duck	500–1000
Goldeneye	<100
Goosander	<100

Also: Mute Swan, Canada Goose, Shelduck
Other birds: passage waders, grebes, terns

Leigh Marsh   *Sheet 178 TQ 8385*
This area includes the marshy Two Tree Island, a Local Nature Reserve which, considering the pressures from boats, fishermen and other disturbance, holds surprisingly high numbers of a variety of species. The numbers of Brent Geese have grown in recent years in line with the national increase and there are strong links with the massive flocks on the Maplin Sands not far away. Wigeon numbers are also good, and waders plentiful.

There are two good vantage points. The first is from the extreme eastern end of Canvey Island. Access to Canvey Island is by the A1301, a turning off the A13 (Grays to Southend) at Great Tarpots. Follow the road through Canvey until it peters out, then walk to the point. Good views of the area can also be had from the front between Westcliff and Leigh-on-Sea though one is looking due south.

WILDFOWL

Brent Goose	1000–5000
Wigeon	1000–2500

Also: Shelduck (100–250), Mallard (100–250), Teal (100–250)

WADERS

Oystercatcher	100–	250
Ringed Plover	250–	500
Grey Plover	250–	500
Turnstone	250–	500
Dunlin	5000–10000	
Knot	1000–	2500
Redshank	1000–	2500
Curlew	500–	1000

North Fambridge, River Crouch   *Sheet 168 TQ 9097*

For most of its length, the River Crouch is too narrow to attract large numbers of water birds. Just downstream from Fambridge, however, it widens out to include an island, Bridgemarsh, once reclaimed, but now rough grazing and saltmarsh. Numbers of wildfowl and waders are small by the standards of some other Essex haunts but are nonetheless interesting and varied.

There is no direct access to the island but footpaths run along the embanked river wall on both sides of the river, and the views from either side are good. The closest approach is via Althorne on the north side. Turn off the B1010 (Latchingdon to Burnham-on-Crouch) road for Althorne Station and cross the railway line. On the south side, footpaths lead to the river from Canewdon. Alternatively one can walk along either bank from North Fambridge and South Fambridge respectively.

WILDFOWL

Brent Goose	250–	500
Shelduck	250–	500
Mallard	100–	500
Teal	500–1000	
Wigeon	500–1000	

Also: Gadwall, Pintail (100–250), Shoveler, Red-breasted Merganser

WADERS

Lapwing	1000–2500
Dunlin	1000–2500

| Redshank | 500–1000 |
| Curlew | 250– 500 |

Also: Ringed Plover, Golden Plover (250–500), Grey Plover, Knot, Bar-tailed Godwit

Stour Estuary   *Sheet 169 TM 2033*

The last of the great Essex estuaries is, in fact, half in Suffolk, but it is dealt with here as, although there is good access on both sides, perhaps the better viewing is on the south side—with the light behind the observer—and slightly more of the birds are found here, too.

The estuary has an area of about 2,200 ha (5,400 acres), of which about 2,000 ha (4,950 acres) is sand and silt flats, with extensive growths of *Zostera* and *Enteromorpha*. This forms the food not just for Brent Geese but also for large numbers of Wigeon, for which this is easily the best site in Essex. These grazing ducks also feed on grass fields, particularly on the north shore, near the head of the estuary. *Hydrobia* is abundant in the mud, helping to feed the considerable numbers of Shelduck, while the whole estuary is an important autumn arrival point for waders coming across the North Sea. There is rather little saltmarsh, about 200 ha (500 acres), as the land rises fairly quickly on either side of the estuary.

On the Essex shore, access can be had at Mistley, on the B1352 (Manningtree to Harwich), where there is one of the largest flocks of Mute Swans in the country. Continuing along the B1352, turn left for Wrabness. Tracks lead from here to the seawall along which runs a public footpath. Turn left for views of Jacques Bay westwards, and right to observe the birds in Copperas Bay and to the east. Parkestone Quay, on the west side of Harwich Harbour, is a good point from which to look back into Copperas Bay.

On the Suffolk shore access is more difficult, although once on the seawall a footpath runs most of the length of the estuary. An important area for wildfowl, Holbrook Bay can be seen from Stutton or Narkstead, reached down a lane from the B1080, a turning off the A137 (Manningtree to Ipswich). Tracks lead to the edge of the river at both localities.

WILDFOWL

Mute Swan	100– 250
Brent Goose	250– 500
Shelduck	1000–2500

Mallard	500–1000
Teal	<100
Wigeon	2500–5000
Pintail	500–1000
Goldeneye	<100

Also: Shoveler, Pochard, Tufted Duck

WADERS

Ringed Plover	100– 250
Grey Plover	250– 500
Lapwing	500–1000
Turnstone	100– 250
Dunlin	10000+
Knot	500–1000
Redshank	2500–5000
Black-tailed Godwit	500–1000
Curlew	500–1000

Also: Golden Plover (100–250), Greenshank, Bar-tailed Godwit

GLOUCESTERSHIRE _____

The county of Gloucestershire lies astride the upper Severn estuary.
This provides the major wetland in the county, though the great tidal
range and fierce currents limit the wildfowl and waders to just two
localities. Elsewhere the county would be almost entirely dry were it
not for the activity of man in excavating gravel pits, which has
produced one major and two minor groups. Near Bourton-on-the-
Water, in the north of the county, there are some small pits which
carry regular small populations of the commoner ducks. The other
smaller group, at Frampton-on-Severn, lies close to the New
Grounds, one of the major estuarine sites, and will be included below
in the description of that area. In the east of the county are the many
pits making up the Cotswold Water Park which is fully covered
below.

Aylburton Warth and Guscar Rocks   *Sheet 162 SO 6098*
This locality is the principal one for waders in the upper estuary and
lies on the west bank just south of Lydney. The waders feed over an
extensive area of the estuary mudflats and concentrate on or near
Guscar Rocks at high tide.

Access is from the A48 (Gloucester to Chepstow), turning off it to
the right, going south, after passing through the village of Alvington,
about 4.8 km (3 miles) south of Lydney. Look for a signpost to
Plusterwine, then continue as far as possible before taking to a
footpath which leads across the railway to the seawall.

WILDFOWL: only relatively small numbers of Shelduck, Wigeon and
other common duck occur here.

WADERS

Ringed Plover	250– 500
Lapwing	1000–2500
Dunlin	1000–2500
Redshank	100– 250
Curlew	500–1000

Also: Turnstone

Cotswold Water Park   *Sheet 163 SU 0596*
This is the name given to the largest group of gravel pits in the
country, currently covering well over 400 ha (1,000 acres) and
scheduled for considerable growth over the next 10–15 years. The
pits vary in size from a hectare or so to over 40, and although many
have various recreational activities taking place on them—including
water-skiing, sailing and fishing—they are extremely attractive to
birds, which can usually find plenty of undisturbed water at any
particular time.

Pochard are very numerous, with substantial numbers of Tufted
Duck as well. Dabbling ducks, too, are present in good numbers,
while other water birds, including Great Crested Grebes, are
plentiful. Freshwater waders drop in on pits where there is exposed
mud at the edges. With new pits appearing all the time, and
conditions changing rapidly in others, numbers of birds are changing
(mainly increasing) all the time. The latest increase has been in
breeding birds, with Tufted Duck joining Great Crested Grebe and
Little Ringed Plover as species breeding in significant numbers.

The Water Park consists of two separate parts: one between Cirencester and Cricklade, to the west of the A419 joining those two towns; the other part mainly to the south of the A417 between Fairford and Lechlade. Virtually all the pits used by wildfowl are adjacent to roads and excellent views can be obtained at quite close range. Because of the continual change taking place in the area with new pits being dug and older ones being taken over for recreation, it is impossible to pinpoint particular ones to visit. In addition, the birds move around depending on disturbance. Instead it is probably best to explore the area and discover its riches for oneself. The western part is clearly signposted off the A419 and there are pits observable from the many lanes leading to the villages of South Cerney, Cerney Wick, Ashton Keynes, Poole Keynes, Somerford Keynes and Shorncote. The eastern pits are smaller in number and carry fewer birds but are still worth exploring, especially those between Fairford and Lechlade reached down the two side roads turning to the right.

WILDFOWL

Mallard	500–1000
Teal	100– 250
Wigeon	250– 500
Pochard	1000–2500
Tufted Duck	500–1000

Also: Goldeneye, Gadwall, Red-crested Pochard
Other birds: passage terns and waders are quite widespread, Great Crested Grebes breed, and large flocks of Coot winter

Although so many of the pits are comparatively recent, the total of Pochard is already one of the highest in Britain.

New Grounds, Slimbridge   *Sheet 162 SO 7205*
Lying at the head of the estuary, this area covers nearly 800 ha (2,000 acres) of mudflats, plus saltmarsh and low-lying grass fields. The Wildfowl Trust has its headquarters here, with the world's largest collection of wildfowl. It manages the whole area as a wildfowl refuge and has built observation towers and many hides from which visitors can obtain excellent views out over the saltmarsh and feeding fields of the wintering geese and ducks without in any way disturbing them. The wintering flock of White-fronted Geese is the largest in the country, while several hundred Bewick's Swans come daily into one of the pens for food, providing a magnificent spectacle. Ducks of

several species abound. Access to the hides is through the Collection, to which an entrance charge is made.

The estuary by the New Grounds is not too good for waders, as the mudbanks are not rich in invertebrates, being scoured by the very strong tides. Some shallow pools have been specially excavated in front of the hides to attract in freshwater species. The only other view possible over the estuary is from Frampton Breakwater at the north end of the New Grounds.

The New Grounds lie beyond the village of Slimbridge which is clearly signposted off the A38 (Gloucester to Bristol) about 19.3 km (12 miles) south of Gloucester. The Wildfowl Trust is open every day except Christmas Day. Frampton Breakwater can be reached through the village of Frampton-on-Severn, on the B4071, a turning off the A38 about 4 miles north of Slimbridge. Take the first left into the village and drive right through it to reach a bridge over the Gloucester ship canal. A footpath leads down to the river from the canal, but first cross over and keep to the right of a tidal creek. Access south from here on to the wildfowl refuge is not permitted.

WILDFOWL

Bewick's Swan	250– 500
White-fronted Goose	2500–5000
Shelduck	100– 250
Mallard	1000–2500
Teal	500–1000
Gadwall	100– 250
Wigeon	1000–2500
Pintail	250– 500
Shoveler	100– 250

Also: every other species of goose on the British list has occurred as vagrant, with Lesser Whitefront, Pinkfoot, Barnacle, Bean almost every year.

WADERS

Ringed Plover	100– 500
Lapwing	1000–2500
Dunlin	1000–2500
Redshank	<100
Curlew	100– 250

Also: Golden Plover (100–250)
Other birds: a Peregrine is present every winter

Just before reaching the turning into Frampton village, the Frampton gravel pits appear on the left of the road. A public footpath starts from some imposing entrance gates on the left of the road and continues round the pits. Diving duck are present in winter in some hundreds, and a wide variety of other species has been recorded.

HAMPSHIRE

The coast of Hampshire is mainly low-lying, and although the conurbations of Southampton and Portsmouth, and industrial complexes such as Fawley, have sterilized some of it, much important wetland habitat remains, particularly in the small estuaries in and to the west of Southampton Water, and in Langstone Harbour further east. The north coast of the Isle of Wight has a number of small estuaries of which only Newton estuary is described below, but the Bembridge Marshes and Brading Harbour at the east end of the island carry a good variety of birds, while smaller numbers of several species will be found in the estuaries of the West Yar and the Medina.

Inland there are many small lakes, together with increasing gravel workings in the north of the county, but none are very important. The only good inland site is the flood plain of the River Avon dealt with below.

Avon Floods   *Sheet 195 SU 1408*
Although this site is included because of its importance to wildfowl, it is necessary to make a strong plea for commonsense from birdwatchers not to attempt to leave the public roads and paths. The area in question is a stretch of flood-meadow alongside the River Avon between Ringwood and Fordingbridge. In normally wet winters the river overflows its banks and creates perfect wildfowl habitat. The principal species, the White-fronted Goose, is particularly sensitive to disturbance from whatever source and only constant wardening and tight restrictions on access preserve the value of the site for geese. With average luck quite a lot can be seen from the roads or tracks and to leave them is to damage geese and goose-watchers alike. A recent threat of drainage is less easy to combat.

The floods lie on the west side of the A338 between Ringwood and

Fordingbridge. Tracks lead off the road at Blashford, while at Ibsley a side road crosses the river at Harbridge.

WILDFOWL

Mute Swan	100– 250
Bewick's Swan	100– 250
White-fronted Goose	500–1000
Mallard	<100
Teal	100– 250
Wigeon	500–1000

Calshot Castle to Fawley   *Sheet 196 SU 4803*

Between Calshot Castle and the vast Fawley refinery there is a fine area of mudflats which so far have not suffered undue pollution or disturbance. They hold useful numbers of several duck species as well as flocks of waders. Access is from the Fawley to Calshot road at Ashlett or, perhaps better, from the Calshot Castle end, when the light will be behind one. It is not practicable to walk the shore between the two points because of the lack of a proper footpath.

WILDFOWL

Shelduck	250– 500
Mallard	100– 250
Teal	500–1000
Wigeon	100– 250
Shoveler	<100
Pochard	<100
Tufted Duck	100– 250

Also: Brent Goose (100–250), Pintail

WADERS

Oystercatcher	250– 500
Ringed Plover	250– 500
Grey Plover	100– 250
Lapwing	500–1000
Turnstone	250– 500
Dunlin	5000+
Redshank	1000–2500

Also: Bar-tailed Godwit

Keyhaven and Pennington Marshes *Sheet 196 SZ 3292*
The stretch of coast between Hurst Castle and the mouth of the River
Lymington has large areas of saltings just outside the seawall, while at
Pennington there is a fine series of lagoons just inside the seawall. A
footpath runs the full length of the coast from Keyhaven village to
Waterford at the mouth of the Lymington, or there is access about
half way along from Pennington village. Duck numbers are mostly
small but there is a good flock of Brent Geese, recently increased, as
well as large population of Dunlin and a mixture of other waders.

WILDFOWL

Brent Goose	250–500
Shelduck	250–500
Teal	250–500
Wigeon	100–250
Red-breasted	
Merganser	<100

Also: Mute Swan, Mallard, Pochard, Goldeneye, Longtail

WADERS

Oystercatcher	<100
Grey Plover	100– 250
Lapwing	500–1000
Dunlin	5000+
Turnstone	<100
Redshank	500–1000
Black-tailed Godwit	<100

Also: Ringed Plover, Bar-tailed Godwit

Langstone Harbour *Sheets 196 and 197 SX 6904*
There are about 1,600 ha (3,950 acres) of rich mud and sand flats in
Langstone Harbour with extensive growths of all three species of
Zostera as well as *Enteromorpha*, plus a further 150 ha (370 acres) of saltmarsh. The latter comprises four islands in the northern part of the
harbour, together with the Farlington Marshes, a tongue projecting
from the north-west corner and consisting of high level grass saltings.
Wader numbers, particularly Dunlin, are very high, with the birds
concentrated on the high salting islands at high tide. At least 40

species of waders have been recorded here in the last 20 years. The most important wildfowl is the Dark-bellied Brent Goose which has shown a dramatic increase here, as elsewhere, in the last seven or eight years. However the increase in Langstone Harbour, as at Chichester Harbour, Sussex, next door, has been greater than the national increase.

Access to Farlington Marshes is from the main A27 south coast trunk road, where it crosses the A2030 to Portsmouth—take the narrow track from the roundabout underneath the flyover. One can walk out along the seawall to the point, on the west side, to view the harbour and the high tide roosts on the little islands off the point of the marshes. Hayling Island is reached by turning south off the A27 at Havant on to the A3023. This also provides good views from points along its west shore, while from the east side the mouth of Chichester Harbour is overlooked. Alternatively, taking the A2030 off the A27 to Eastney brings one to the west side of the harbour mouth.

WILDFOWL

Brent Goose	2500–5000
Shelduck	1000–2500
Mallard	<100
Teal	500–1000
Wigeon	1000–2500
Pintail	<100
Shoveler	<100
Goldeneye	<100
Red-breasted	
Merganser	<100

Also: Mute Swan, Gadwall, Long-tailed Duck

WADERS

Oystercatcher	500–1000
Ringed Plover	250– 500
Grey Plover	250– 500
Turnstone	<100
Dunlin	10000+
Knot	250– 500
Redshank	1000–2500
Black-tailed Godwit	250– 500
Bar-tailed Godwit	100– 250

Also: Lapwing (500–1,000), Greenshank
Other birds: a long list of rarities and less common species have been observed here. Grebes and terns are regular.

Needs Oar Point Sheet 196 SX 4397
The Hampshire and Isle of Wight Naturalists' Trust manages this coastal area as a reserve and access is by permit only. It is perhaps best known for its vast (20,000 pairs) colony of Black-headed Gulls in which Mediterranean Gulls have bred. In winter it carries a wide variety of duck and waders though numbers are not great. It can be reached by following the lane south from Bucklers Hard, which lies just south of Beaulieu. Just after a sharp right turn at St Leonards, a track leads coastwards past a farm. There is room to park at the end.

WILDFOWL

Mallard	250– 500
Teal	250– 500
Wigeon	500–1000
Pintail	<100
Shoveler	<100

Also: Brent Goose, Shelduck, Pochard, Goldeneye

WADERS

Lapwing	1000–2500
Dunlin	250– 500
Turnstone	<100

Also: Oystercatcher (100–250), Ringed Plover, Grey Plover, Redshank (100–250)

Newtown Marsh, Isle of Wight Sheet 196 SX 4291
This estuary complex covers about 250 ha (620 acres), of which a central area of about 53 ha (130 acres) was created when a seawall was breached in 1954 and never repaired. Numbers of birds using the area noticeably increased after this. The old seawall provides a raised walk giving excellent views over the mudflats and saltmarshes and is accessible from the village of Newtown. This is reached down lanes from the A3054 (Newport to Yarmouth) road.

WILDFOWL

Brent Goose	250–500
Shelduck	250–500
Teal	250–500
Wigeon	250–500
Pintail	100–250

Also: Canada Goose (100–250), Mallard, Goldeneye, Red-breasted Merganser

WADERS

Lapwing	500–1000
Dunlin	1000–2500
Black-tailed Godwit	100– 250

Also: Oystercatcher, Ringed Plover, Grey Plover, Turnstone, Redshank (100–250)

HEREFORD
AND WORCESTER ⸺

Although covering a considerable area, these two counties, now joined together, lack any freshwater body of any size, whether lakes, reservoirs or gravel pits. The rivers Severn, Avon and Wye flow through them but only rarely flood to provide good conditions for waterfowl. The Barnt Green (Bittell) reservoirs south of Birmingham are probably the best wetlands in the county, with peaks of a few hundred Mallard and Pochard, together with smaller flocks of Teal, Wigeon and Tufted Duck.

1   Bar-tailed Godwits are winter visitors to Britain from Russia. They typically feed on the tide edge, wading in shallow water.

2   Six Pintail and a Mallard dabbling in the edge of the tide. Large flocks of Pintail are only found in rather few localities.

3 An aerial view of the western end of the Swale, Kent. The creek-dissected saltmarsh in the foreground provides breeding sites, feeding grounds and high tide roosts for a variety of species.

4 Highland lochs, with stony shores and little emergent vegetation, are not very attractive to wildfowl.

5 Dark-bellied Brent Geese swimming at high tide off Leigh-on-Sea, Essex. After 25 years of protection they have become quite tame in most of their east and south coast wintering haunts.

6 Pochard, and a few Tufted Duck, on Barn Elms reservoir, London. The London reservoirs together form one of the most important haunts in Britain for these two species.

7 Up to 60,000 Greylag Geese winter in Scotland. They feed on farmland, spending the night on secluded lochs, large reservoirs or estuaries.

8 Short-grass saltmarsh provides feeding for grazing geese and ducks, such as Barnacle Geese and Wigeon, as well as nesting sites for Lapwing and Redshank.

9 At low tide wading birds spread out to feed over the mudflats; the edges of muddy creeks are favoured sites for several species.

10 Pink-footed Geese winter in many of the same areas of Scotland as Greylags, but also occur in Lancashire, Humberside and around the Wash.

11 Formerly restricted entirely to feeding in the inter-tidal zone, Dark-bellied Brent Geese have taken to feeding, in recent years, on farmland just inside the sea wall.

12 The majestic power of Whooper Swans in flight. Those wintering in northern Britain breed in Iceland. The small numbers wintering in East Anglia come from Scandinavia and Russia.

13   Red-breasted Mergansers (seen here) and Goosanders are common only in northern England and Scotland, but small numbers of both species occur in winter on reservoirs and estuaries further south.

14   The long bill of the Goosander is not only hooked but also has serrations down each side to help it grasp the fish on which it feeds.

15 On the northern edge of the Firth of Tay, Scotland, is an extensive belt of reeds favoured by dabbling ducks, especially Teal.

16 Part of the large resident population of Eider Ducks to be seen on the Ythan estuary, north of Aberdeen.

17 Shelducks over a flooded saltmarsh. They breed on most low-lying coasts of Britain and winter flocks occur in all the major estuaries.

18 Barnacle Geese winter on the Solway Firth, and on Islay and other Hebridean islands. They graze on saltmarsh and on grass fields within a few miles of their estuarine roosts.

19 Oystercatchers can be found both on estuaries and on rocky coasts. Their food includes bivalves and softer invertebrates.

20 The Purple Sandpiper is among the tamest of waders. They are found in small numbers scattered round most of Britain's rocky coasts.

HERTFORDSHIRE _____

Without the man-made construction of some small canal feeder reservoirs near Tring, Hertfordshire would be without a wetland of any importance. It is comparatively small, includes chalk downland and has no river or natural lake of any size. There are gravel pits in some areas, notably on the Essex border near Broxbourne and in the south-west at Rickmansworth, and these carry useful numbers of typical species.

Tring Reservoirs   *Sheet 165 SP 9113*
The reservoirs, a National Nature Reserve, lie near the B489 (Aston Clinton to Ivinghoe). Aston Clinton is midway between Aylesbury and Tring on the A41. Excellent views of all four waters can be had from the roads and from footpaths.

WILDFOWL

Mallard	100–500
Teal	100–250
Shoveler	100–250
Pochard	100–250
Tufted Duck	100–250

Also: Bewick's Swan, Greylag Goose, Wigeon, Goosander
Other birds: Great Crested Grebe, passage waders including shanks and sandpipers, and passage terns

HUMBERSIDE _____

This new county is centred on the Humber estuary, formed by the rivers Trent and Ouse plus about five smaller streams. There are very important wildfowl and wader haunts along its length and these will be dealt with here. Elsewhere there is little to attract birds to the flat sandy coast devoid of inlets. There is one freshwater wetland of importance, Hornsea Mere, also covered below, but inland there is merely a long history of drainage destroying marshes and flood-meadows and gradually clearing the area of wetlands. The only remaining floodland is on the River Derwent which forms the border between Humberside and North Yorkshire and it is dealt with under the latter county.

Hornsea Mere   *Sheet 107 TA 1947*
Lying within a couple of miles of the sea, just behind the village of Hornsea, this natural lake is rich in both breeding and wintering wildfowl, and is noted for its breeding warblers as well as its attractiveness to passing migrants of a wide variety of species. The total area, including large reedbeds, is about 230 ha (570 acres), of which about 120 ha (300 acres) is open water. The lake is quite shallow, averaging about 3.4 m (11 ft) in depth, and is eutrophic. The surrounding vegetation forms a rich fen community with plenty of emergent vegetation and a good insect life. The RSPB manage the lake as a reserve.

There is a car park and excellent viewpoint on the west side, reached from Hornsea village. The B1244 (Hornsea to Leven) runs along the north side and the Mere can be seen quite well from a number of places.

WILDFOWL

Mallard	1000–2500
Teal	100– 250
Gadwall	100– 250
Wigeon	250– 500
Shoveler	100– 250
Pochard	500–1000
Tufted Duck	250– 500
Goldeneye	100– 250

Also: Mute Swan, Canada Goose, Pintail
Other birds: passage waders and terns, breeding warblers

Humber Estuary   *Sheets 106, 107 & 113 SE 9622-TA 3616*
On the north side of the estuary, between Hull and Spurn Point, there are about 6,000 ha (15,000 acres) of mudflats backed by fringing saltmarsh. Not all this is of high value but about a third, in the area

between Sunk Island and Kilnsea, is quite rich in invertebrates and so attracts good numbers of waders and wildfowl, with Mallard, Shelduck, Dunlin and Knot predominating. Side roads from the A1033 (Hull to Withernsea) lead down towards the shore at Sunk Island and Old Hall from which access can be gained to the seawall. The B1445 leaves the A1033 at Patrington for Kilnsea, and side roads or tracks lead to points on the coast to the west of Kilnsea.

Further west, upstream of Hull, there is a second and more important area for birds, centred on the Humber Wildfowl Refuge. The latter covers just over 1,215 ha (3,000 acres) and stretches virtually from bank to bank between Brough and Whitton Ness in the east to Faxfleet in the west. It was afforded statutory protection in 1955 primarily to safeguard the roost of Pink-footed Geese which were present in many thousands. Although the geese have become much reduced in recent years, the refuge now harbours significant numbers of several duck and wader species. Further downstream on the south side is Read's Island, formerly a major Pinkfoot roost and still the haunt of duck.

The north side of the upper estuary can be viewed from Faxfleet—at the end of a turning off the main A63 (Selby to Hull) at Scalby; from Broomfleet—take any of the turnings between Newport and South Cave; and from Brough—down turnings at Elloughton or Welton. Access to the refuge is prohibited under the by-laws. On the south side the A1077 (Scunthorpe to Barton-on-Humber) skirts the shore opposite Read's Island just west of South Feriby, while side roads further west lead to Winteringham and Whitton, both virtually on the coast.

The wildfowl and wader numbers for the whole estuary are combined in the tables below. The great bulk of most wildfowl species occur in the upper estuary, above Hull, while the waders are more evenly split. There are also fairly small numbers of waders on the south side just west of Grimsby.

WILDFOWL

Pink-footed Goose	500–1000
Shelduck	500–1000
Mallard	2500–5000
Teal	500–1000
Wigeon	1000–2500

WADERS

Oystercatcher	1000–2500
Lapwing	1000–2500
Dunlin	10000+
Knot	10000+
Sanderling	250– 500
Turnstone	250– 500
Redshank	1000–2500
Curlew	1000–2500

Also: Curlew Sandpiper, Ruff, Whimbrel, Bar-tailed Godwit (100–250)
Other birds: diver, terns
Note that Pinkfeet were formerly much more common, with late autumn peaks of up to 10,000 birds in the late 1950s, and 5,000–6,000 staying through the winter. The decline has been linked with changing conditions in Scotland where there is now better protection and more food. However, a recent return to two other English haunts, Southport in Lancashire and the Wash, has not been paralleled on the Humber.

KENT _____

The south and east coasts of Kent are lacking in good wetland habitat, while former fresh marshes along the small river valleys have been drained out of existence. Pegwell and Sandwich Bays hold small numbers of birds, though disturbance is rather high. Up the Stour valley from here is the colliery subsidence of Stodmarsh, the richest inland site in the county. The north coast, by contrast, has large areas of excellent estuarine habitat, and although some has been lost in recent years to industrial development, and more has been threatened, other parts are now safeguarded by reserve status. The Swale and the Medway estuaries are particularly important. The Thames-side North Kent Marshes from the Medway to Gravesend are also of considerable value. Further up the Thames there are increasing flocks of wildfowl and waders as the waters are cleaned up.

Gravel pits and private lakes provide the only inland water of the county apart from Stodmarsh. The pits at Sevenoaks have been the site of a long-term and very successful experiment in improving such workings for wildfowl and other birds.

Inner Thames   *Sheet 177 TQ 4881*
Above Gravesend the Thames narrows considerably but there are still stretches of saltings and mudflats for waders on both sides of the river, while ducks, especially diving ducks, have been increasing fast in recent years, probably gaining from the reduction in pollution that has taken place. The best area is probably Thamesmead on the Kent shore between Erith and Woolwich. Access to the shore is not easy though a path runs along the bank for most of this stretch.

WILDFOWL

Mute Swan	100– 250
Shelduck	250– 500
Mallard	500–1000
Teal	250– 500
Pintail	100– 250
Pochard	1000–2500
Tufted Duck	100– 250

Also: Shoveler

WADERS

Ringed Plover	100– 250
Grey Plover	100– 250
Lapwing	250– 500
Dunlin	5000+
Redshank	500–1000

Also: Knot, Curlew

Medway Marshes   *Sheet 178 TQ 8670*
The estuary of the River Medway stretches about 16 km (10 miles) inland but the part which is of greatest value to wildfowl and waders is restricted to the mudflats and saltmarsh on the south side between Gillingham and the junction of the Medway with the Swale at Queenborough. Here there are about 670 ha (1,660 acres) of marshland, much of it in the form of high-tide islands of saltings.
  Although the area is complex and much of it difficult to see, the

bird-watching is excellent at a number of points. The first of these involves walking along the west bank of the Chetney peninsula starting at Chetney Cottages. The latter are on a lane reached by turning off the A249 (Sittingbourne to Sheppey) at Iwade. The road from Chetney Cottages to Lower Halstow via Barksore runs along the shore of the estuary, though reclamation has caused the shore to retreat from the road and access is no longer so close. Finally, from Lower Halstow make for Ham Green near Upchurch whence a track leads down to the seawall.

On the north side of the estuary, Stoke Ooze is a good area, viewed from sea walls close to Stoke Lagoon, see North Kent Marshes.

WILDFOWL

Brent Goose	500–	1000
Shelduck	1000–	2500
Mallard	250–	500
Teal	2500–	5000
Wigeon	5000–	10000
Pintail	500–	1000
Shoveler	100–	250
Goldeneye	<100	

Also: Bewick's Swan, White-fronted Goose, Pochard, Tufted Duck, Red-breasted Merganser

WADERS

Oystercatcher	500–	1000
Ringed Plover	500–	1000
Grey Plover	500–	1000
Lapwing	1000–	2500
Turnstone	<100	
Dunlin	5000–	10000
Knot	500–	1000
Redshank	1000–	2500
Spotted Redshank	100–	250
Greenshank	<100	
Black-tailed Godwit	250–	500
Curlew	1000–	2500

Also: Golden Plover (100–250), Curlew Sandpiper, Ruff, Bar-tailed Godwit, Whimbrel
Other birds: divers, grebes

North Kent Marshes *Sheet 179 TQ 8080*

The Thames-side marshes along the north Kent coast from the Isle of Grain west to beyond Cliffe have suffered from reclamation and industrialization but have also gained from the digging of clay pits, and much excellent habitat remains. Starting at the east end, the first of the three sections of this area lies between Grain and Allhallows, taking in Yantlet Creek. This has a good wader roost and a fair number of ducks, as well as some White-fronted Geese. To the west lies the High Halstow Marshes and St Mary's and Egypt Bays. This stretch carries good numbers of ducks and Whitefronts and was formerly the best part of the area. However, it has been superseded in recent years by the most westerly section, from Egypt Bay to Cliffe which, together with the clay pits at Cliffe, holds the largest numbers of most wildfowl species.

The head of Yantlet Creek can be reached on foot along a disused railway line leading from the A228 (Rochester to Isle of Grain) just past a level-crossing outside the village of Lower Stoke. When the track reaches the creek it is possible either to cross over to the east bank and round the Isle of Grain or to stay on the west bank where Stoke Lagoon is well worth visiting.

The High Halstow and Egypt Bay section can be reached from the village of High Halstow. Coming from Rochester, three lanes lead to the village from the A228. Passing through the village, take the Decoy Hill Road to the left, past the RSPB reserve of Northward Hill wood, until the road ends. Then walk to the seawall and turn east for St Mary's Bay and west for Egypt Bay.

From Egypt Bay it is possible to walk right round the coast to Cliffe and its clay pits. Alternatively one can drive to Cliffe from High Halstow, or direct from Rochester down the B2000, taking the car through the village as far as it is possible to go, to the coastguard cottages, then walk to the shore with the pits on the left. It is also possible to walk right round the pits.

WILDFOWL

White-fronted Goose	500–1000
Shelduck	1000–2500
Mallard	500–1000
Teal	100– 500
Wigeon	500–1000
Pintail	100– 250

Shoveler	100– 250
Pochard	100– 250
Tufted Duck	100– 250

Also: Mute Swan (100–250), Bewick's Swan, Brent Goose (100–250), Gadwall, Goldeneye

WADERS

Grey Plover	<100
Dunlin	1000–2500
Redshank	250– 500
Curlew	500–1000

Also: Ringed Plover, Turnstone, Knot (100–250), Bar-tailed Godwit

Stodmarsh   *Sheet 179 TR 2061*

This mining subsidence covers about 375 ha (900 acres) and contains extensive reedbeds and pools, with further periodic flooding of adjacent meadows. It is most noted for its breeding birds, including at least six species of duck. Wintering wildfowl are not very numerous but of good diversity. A wide variety of other bird species occurs, at all times of the year.

A track leads out of the village of Stodmarsh on to a bank which crosses the marsh, giving good views on either side. Stodmarsh village can be approached off the A28 (Canterbury to Margate) by turning right at Sturry or Upstreet. Alternatively there is a public footpath along the north bank of the Great Stour River, accessible from Fordwich at the west end and Upstreet at the east.

WILDFOWL

Mute Swan	<100
Mallard	250–500
Teal	100–250
Gadwall	<100
Wigeon	<100
Shoveler	100–250
Pochard	100–250
Tufted Duck	<100

The Swale *Sheets 178 & 179 TQ 9666*

This is a broad tidal channel separating the Isle of Sheppey from the mainland. There are about 2,000 ha (5,000 acres) of mudflats which are more extensive on the southern side and contain a rich invertebrate fauna. On the north side there are considerable areas of wet grassland and marsh with a great variety of breeding birds, including no less than eight species of duck. In addition there are shell banks, coastal lagoons and sheltered arms of water. White-fronted and Brent Geese winter, and both ducks and waders are present in large numbers.

There are several good points of access to the Swale, and most of the south side can be seen very well. The north side is more difficult to work. Starting in the south-east and working round clockwise, the first locality is Seasalter, a village on an unclassified road just west of Whitstable turning off the A299 (Whitstable to Faversham) just outside the town. The road runs along the coast here, west towards Graveney, while a footpath continues west along the seawall when the road turns inland.

Continuing on the road to Graveney, turn right in the village and down to the seawall, from which it is possible to walk back to Seasalter. From the centre of Faversham, a lane leads down to Oare and the South Harty Ferry. Footpaths continue along the seawall westwards to Conyer, or this village can be reached by road, turning off the main A2 (Faversham to Sittingbourne) at Teynham. The section from Conyer to Sittingbourne can be covered either by walking west from Conyer or by taking another unclassified turning north off the A2 at Bapchild to Little Murston and then walking.

Crossing over onto the Isle of Sheppey on the A249, footpaths lead down to Emley from just north of Kingsferry Bridge, and to the shore from Brambledown on the A250. Between Eastchurch and Leysdown on the A250 a lane leads down to Harty Ferry and it is possible to walk both west and east from here along the seawall. Finally, continuing through to Leysdown, turn south for Shellness; there is a nature reserve on the point with restricted access, while a National Nature Reserve covers other areas on the north side, again with no access.

WILDFOWL

White-fronted Goose	500–1000
Brent Goose	1000–2500
Shelduck	1000–2500

Mallard	500–1000
Teal	250– 500
Wigeon	2500–5000
Pintail	<100
Shoveler	100– 250
Tufted Duck	<100
Red-breasted Merganser	<100

Also: Goldeneye

WADERS

Oystercatcher	2500–5000
Ringed Plover	100– 250
Golden Plover	500–1000
Grey Plover	500–1000
Lapwing	1000–2500
Turnstone	250– 500
Dunlin	5000+
Knot	2500–5000
Redshank	500–1000
Black-tailed Godwit	250– 500
Bar-tailed Godwit	500–1000
Curlew	500–1000

Also: Sanderling, Spotted Redshank, Greenshank, Whimbrel
Other birds: raptors, skuas

LANCASHIRE

Lancashire is blessed with two of the finest estuaries in the country, Morecambe Bay in the north, which it shares with Cumbria, and the Ribble. Inland there is not much water attractive to wildfowl, with the exception of Martin Mere, lying behind Southport and not far from the Ribble, and Leighton Moss, close to Morecambe Bay. The various inland lakes and reservoirs hold rather few ducks. As well as ducks and waders, very large flocks of Pink-footed Geese occur in the county and can be found feeding on the mosses (flat, rich farmland) behind Formby and Southport and also further north around the mouth of the River Lune.

Leighton Moss   *Sheet 97 SD 4875*

Once drained and ploughed but then allowed to reflood about 60 years ago, Leighton Moss, an area of about 135 ha (330 acres), is now extensively overgrown with reeds, and perhaps less attractive to wildfowl than it once was. However, it is very important as a breeding site for many marshland birds and is managed as a reserve by the RSPB. Shooting is still carried on in the winter and the reserve is not then open to the public. However a public footpath crosses the area and a bird-watching hide, open throughout the year, has been sited on it. Summer visits, April to September, are by permit from the warden, Myers Farmhouse, Silverdale, Carnforth, Lancs.

The public footpath, which follows a raised causeway, starts at Silverdale station, which is just through the village, reached down unclassified roads from Carnforth on the A6 or Arnside on the B5282.

WILDFOWL

Mallard	500–1000
Teal	500–1000
Pintail	100– 250
Shoveler	100– 500

Also: Gadwall, Wigeon, Tufted Duck, Pochard, Goldeneye
Other birds: breeding bids, including Bittern and warblers, passage waders, terns and raptors

Martin Mere   *Sheet 108 SD 4214*

Lying just behind Southport, this was formerly a very large lake but was more or less completely drained in the past leaving an area of winter flooding. This was very attractive to wildfowl but was quite heavily shot until very recently. However its purchase by the Wildfowl Trust in 1969 and the cessation of shooting has allowed its potential to be better appreciated and the flooded area, deliberately increased, now carries very large numbers of ducks, and sometimes acts as an alternative roost for the Pinkfeet of the Southport Sands. There are public hides overlooking a permanent pool, and over the

water and wet fields of the Mere accessible from within the
Wildfowl Trust enclosures, to which there is an entrance fee. Martin
Mere is signposted from the B5246 which runs between Rufford on
the A59 (Preston to Ormskirk) and the A565 (Preston to Southport)
road.

WILDFOWL

Mallard	2500– 5000
Teal	5000–10000
Wigeon	1000– 2500
Pintail	1000– 2500
Gadwall	100– 250
Pochard	<100
Tufted Duck	<100
Shoveler	<100

Other birds: passage waders and wintering Ruff, raptors
One of the best sites for Teal in the country

Morecambe Bay   *Sheets 97 & 102 SD 4070*
Formed from the estuaries of several rivers, but particularly the
Wyre, Lune, Kent and Leven, Morecambe Bay covers more than 260
sq km (100 sq miles) and is far more attractive to waders than to
wildfowl. At a winter peak over 200,000 waders may be present, with
the largest numbers of Knot, Dunlin, Sanderling, Ringed Plover, and
Oystercatcher in the country, and significant numbers of several
other species.
    In such an enormous area it is a question of finding the spots where
the birds are likely to concentrate, such as high-tide roosts and
favoured feeding spots. Going anti-clockwise round the bay, one
starts at Knott End-on-Sea down the B5377 off the A588 (Blackpool
to Lancaster) at Preesall. From here one can walk to Pilling along the
coast. Pilling is a good area for waders and for Pinkfeet and can be
reached by turning off further along the A588. Just north of
Cockerham on the A588 a lane leads left to Bank End, while another
good place is Glasson on the B5270, another turning off the A588. For
viewing the stretch from Morecambe to Hest Bank, the A589 and
A5105 roads run close to the shore, while at Hest Bank it is possible to
pass under the railway line and follow a track beside the saltings.

Walking north from here takes one towards the mouth of the River Keer and a very extensive tract of saltings.

The north side of the estuary can be approached from the village of Silverdale, by turning off the A6 at Carnforth onto unclassified roads to reach it. Minor roads or tracks lead to the coast both north and south of the village.

The Kent estuary is the next feature and this can be very well seen from the B5282 (Arnside to Milnthorpe) on the south side. The north side is less accessible but the road from Grange-over-Sands to Meathop runs close to the estuary and a footpath leads down to the shore. The north-western arm of the bay is the Leven estuary which is best seen from the west shore. Minor roads lead from the A590 in and just north of Ulverston and reach the shore at Plumpton Hall and Canal Foot. It is also worth walking north from Bardsea which lies on the A5087 south of Ulverston, or driving south to Rampside. Finally go through Barrow and turn left on to Walney Island.

WILDFOWL: good counts of wildfowl for Morecambe Bay are not available but certainly several hundreds of Mallard, Teal and Wigeon occur, as do Shelduck. Pink-footed Geese reach 2,500 in the Pilling/Cockerham area, especially late in the winter. Merganser and Goosander are certainly present in some numbers.

WADERS

Oystercatcher	25000+
Ringed Plover	5000–10000
Golden Plover	1000– 2500
Grey Plover	100– 250
Lapwing	2500– 5000
Turnstone	1000– 2500
Dunlin	25000+
Knot	50000+
Sanderling	5000–10000
Bar-tailed Godwit	5000–10000
Curlew	10000–25000

Also: Purple Sandpiper, Curlew Sandpiper, Greenshank
Other birds: divers, seabirds
Oystercatcher (23% of British total), Ringed Plover (32%), Dunlin (9%), Knot (25%), Sanderling (40%) and Bar-tailed Godwit (33%) are all present in greater numbers at peak than anywhere else in Britain.

Ribble Estuary   *Sheet 102 SD 4026*

The Ribble estuary, including the very extensive sandflats at its
mouth, forms one of the 10 largest sand-silt flats in the country, with
over 5,800 ha (14,300 acres), together with one of the largest
continuous saltmarshes of 2,800 ha (6,900 acres). Small wonder, then,
that it is also extremely attractive to wildfowl and waders, with both
a great diversity and very large numbers.

The Pink-footed Geese roosting on the Southport Sands near the
mouth of the Ribble can be found scattered over a wide area of rich
farmland during the day, but particularly on the 'mosses' between the
A567 and A565 roads. Driving along the many connecting lanes in the
rectangle of Southport, Scarisbrick, Hawkayne and Formby, one is
virtually guaranteed sightings of large flocks, which are often
surprisingly approachable, using the car as a hide. This is especially
true during November and December when numbers are at their
peak. Only the flatness of the ground hinders observation but
judicious use of slight rises and railway bridges can overcome this,
while flying birds should be followed to show where there are
feeding flocks on the ground.

The Ribble estuary has footpaths on either bank and it is possible to
walk for many rewarding miles. On the south side the footpath runs
from Crossens, a suburb of Southport, lying to its north on the A565
(Preston). Turn left here coming from Southport and head for
Crossens Pool, then walk to Marsh Farm before the seawall turns
back inland to go round a creek. Alternatively, follow the
unclassified road from Crossens to Hundred End and Hesketh Bank,
both places giving access to the coastal footpath. On the north side of
the estuary the coastal path can be picked up at Freckleton at the east
end, and Lytham in the west. Freckleton village is on the A584
(Preston to Lytham) about six miles from each. A lane leads through
the village to the shore. One can then walk west from here to
Lytham. Alternatively, starting at Lytham, there is a good view from
the promenade over the mudflats at the mouth of the estuary, and
then a footpath leading eastwards past Warton Marsh to Freckleton.

WILDFOWL

Pink-footed Goose	10000–20000
Bewick's Swan	100– 250
Shelduck	1000– 2500
Mallard	1000– 2500
Teal	1000– 2500

Wigeon	2500– 5000
Common Scoter	250– 500
Pintail	1000– 2500

Also: Whooper Swan, White-fronted Goose, Gadwall, Shoveler (100–250), Goldeneye, Velvet Scoter

WADERS

Oystercatcher	2500– 5000
Ringed Plover	500– 1000
Golden Plover	1000– 2500
Grey Plover	500– 1000
Lapwing	2500– 5000
Turnstone	250– 500
Dunlin	25000+
Knot	50000+
Sanderling	5000–10000
Black-tailed Godwit	500– 1000
Bar-tailed Godwit	5000–10000
Redshank	2500– 5000
Curlew	500– 1000

Also: Curlew Sandpiper, Little Stint, Ruff, Greenshank, Whimbrel
  Pinkfeet, Mallard, Pintail, Dunlin, Knot, Sanderling and Bar-tailed Godwit are all present in numbers exceeded at only a very few other sites.

LEICESTERSHIRE _____

The inland county of Leicestershire would hold rather few wildfowl were it not for the several reservoirs which have been built within its boundaries. Cropston and Swithland reservoirs just north-west of Leicester, together with Thornton and Blackbroom reservoirs a little further west, carry moderate numbers of the common ducks, as do Knipton reservoir and the fishponds at Belvoir in the north-east corner of the county. In the south-east corner lies Eyebrook reservoir, which qualifies for detailed treatment, as does the brand new and very large Rutland Water.

Eyebrook Reservoir   *Sheet 141 SP 8596*
About 160 ha (400 acres) in extent and up to 13 m (40 ft) in depth,
Eyebrook reservoir has benefited from long protection, with only
summer trout-fishing to disturb the birds. Wintering wildfowl are
both plentiful and varied while, when there are mud areas exposed,
waders are frequent.

The reservoir can be reached from the A6003 (Uppingham to
Corby) road. Coming from Uppingham, take the first turning on the
right to Stoke Dry and come to the reservoir shortly after passing
through the village. This road leads round the upper end of the
reservoir, giving good views, and then, by turning left, carries on
down the west side, again with good viewing from the road. Entry to
the reservoir is both strictly prohibited and unnecessary.

WILDFOWL

Canada Goose	<100
Mallard	1000–2500
Teal	250– 500
Wigeon	500–1000
Pochard	250– 500
Tufted Duck	100– 250
Goldeneye	<100
Goosander	<100

Also: Mute Swan, Bewick's Swan, Shoveler

Rutland Water   *Sheet 141 SK 9307*
This massive reservoir, of over 1,215 ha (3,000 acres) is included here
on its potential as flooding has only just been completed. Already up
to 2,000 Mallard and several hundred each of Pochard and Tufted
Duck have been counted there and clearly it will be a most valuable
area for such ducks in the future. Part of the northern arm of this Y-
shaped water has been designated a nature reserve and bird-watchers
will be allowed to use hides. However arrangements are not yet
complete. A general tour of the area should produce some good views
over the water from the many lanes round the reservoir, and when
there are facilities for bird-watchers these will be sign-posted.

The reservoir lies just east of Oakham and is signposted off the
A606 to Stamford or the A6003 to Uppingham.

LINCOLNSHIRE ⸺⸺⸺

Now that the new county of Humbersic has removed the south shore of the Humber estuary from Lincolnshire, the latter is left with the Wash as its sole major wetland. It shares this with Norfolk but the whole area is dealt with here for convenience. Inland Lincolnshire is a dry county, with small lakes and gravel pits but none of importance.

The Wash   *Sheets 122, 131 & 132 TF 5040*

The vast indentation is fringed with saltmarsh along many stretches of its coast, and has very extensive exposed mud and sandflats at low tide. High-tide bird-watching is well nigh essential in most places. The Wash is second in importance only to Morecambe Bay for waders, while certain wildfowl, especially Shelduck, Wigeon and Brent Geese, are very numerous. It is not an easy place to watch birds as points of access are few in some areas and visibility restricted by lack of elevation. At high tide, though, some enormous roosts of waders assemble, sometimes on fields just inland of the seawall if the saltings are covered, providing a marvellous spectacle. Co-ordinated counts which have demonstrated the great value of the area have been made in recent years.

Going clockwise round the Wash, one starts at Snettisham on the A149 (Hunstanton to King's Lynn) where a lane leads down to the beach where there is a holiday bungalow development. Park here and walk southwards along the beach, to bring you past a chain of gravel pits just inland, run as a reserve by the RSPB. There are hides overlooking the southernmost pit. The next stretch of coast, from Wolferton to Wootton, and the mouth of the River Ouse, is a particularly important one, though difficult to get at. A footpath runs along the top of the seawall from King's Lynn (make for the old lighthouse near the mouth of the river on the east bank) past North Wootton and Wolferton, where it can be reached via farm tracks.

The section from the Ouse to the Nene River also involves walking along the seawall. This can be reached first down lanes from West Lynn, a village on the A17 (King's Lynn to Boston) just west of the Ouse, or turning right just before Terrington St Clement towards Ongar Hill. At the other end, the Nene mouth is approached down a lane on the east bank which goes as far as the old lighthouse which once marked the entrance to the river but is now well inland. A path continues along the seawall and round the point to the Ouse.

Access to the next stretch, from the Nene to the Welland, is made more difficult by successive reclamations which make maps and paths quite quickly out of date. The best approach is probably from the B1359 which leaves the A17 at Chapelgate, west of Long Sutton, and runs down to Gedney Drove End. Lanes to Dawsmere and Holbeach St Matthews eventually give way to tracks and paths leading to the seawall.

Crossing the Welland and joining the A16 for Boston, turn right just south of that town for Wyboston, going through this to near Roads Farm. From here one can walk to Frampton Marsh and Boston Point on the south side of the mouth of the River Witham.

The west coast of the Wash has the A52 (Boston to Skegness) running parallel with it, and between Boston and Wrangle a veritable maze of lanes lead through villages such as Fishtoft and Frieston to find their way to the seawall. If in doubt, head eastwards. From Wrangle northwards there are no villages between the A52 and the Wash, only tracks leading to farms or to RAF observation towers on the seawall. There are bombing targets offshore but activity is more or less confined to weekdays. Most of several right-hand turnings off the A52 will lead down to the shore.

Finally, at the north end of this long coast there is Gibraltar Point Bird Observatory overlooking the north end of Wainfleet Sands. The observatory can be reached from Skegness seafront, taking a road southwards past the golf course.

WILDFOWL

Bewick's Swan	<100
Pink-footed Goose	2500– 5000
Brent Goose	5000–10000
Shelduck	10000+
Mallard	1000– 2500
Teal	100– 500
Wigeon	5000–10000
Pintail	250– 500
Shoveler	100– 500
Tufted Duck	<100
Goldeneye	100– 250
Eider	100– 250
Common Scoter	1000– 2500

Velvet Scoter	<100
Longtail	<100
Red-breasted	
Merganser	<100

Also: Pochard, Scaup

WADERS

Oystercatcher	10000+
Ringed Plover	500– 1000
Golden Plover	500– 1000
Grey Plover	2500– 5000
Turnstone	500– 1000
Dunlin	25000+
Knot	50000+
Sanderling	1000– 2500
Redshank	5000–10000
Greenshank	100– 250
Black-tailed Godwit	<100
Bar-tailed Godwit	2500– 5000
Curlew	5000–10000
Whimbrel	100– 250

Also: Curlew Sandpiper, Little Stint, Spotted Redshank
Other birds: raptors, skuas
Shelduck (18% of British total), Grey Plover (22%), Dunlin (7%), Knot (25%) and Redshank (7%) are all either the highest or second highest levels in the country.

LONDON _____

The drinking water reservoirs of Greater London total well over 1,400 ha (3,500 acres) and vary in size from 40 ha (100 acres) to over 290 ha (700 acres). Although most of them have artificial banks, they have proved very attractive to ducks, particularly the diving species, and between them hold significant numbers of Pochard and Tufted Duck. The birds move around according to the availability of their required foods and reservoirs may come into favour and then fall out again over a period of years. Access to virtually all the reservoirs is restricted to permit holders only. Permits may be obtained from the Metropolitan Water Board, New River Head, Rosebery Avenue, London EC1.

Barn Elms Reservoir   *Sheet 176 TQ 2377*

Apart from the lakes in the London parks, this reservoir is the closest standing water to the centre of London. It is situated on the south bank of the Thames just east of Hammersmith Bridge. The flock of Gadwall is a feature not shared by other reservoirs. Access is by permit only and is from the road leaving the south end of Hammersmith Bridge going eastwards.

WILDFOWL

Gadwall	100– 250
Pochard	500–1000
Tufted Duck	500–1000

Also: Mallard (100–250), Teal (100–250), Shoveler, Wigeon

Datchet Reservoir   *Sheet 176 TQ 0177*

This is the most westerly of the large reservoirs, lying right beside the M4 just south of Slough. It has only recently been completed and it is too early to give any counts for the numbers of ducks, but its considerable size suggests it will be of some importance to them.

Lea Valley Reservoir—Walthamstow, William Girling
and King George V   *Sheet 177 TQ 3790*

A whole chain of reservoirs has been created in the Lea Valley in north-east London. The best of them are the Walthamstow reservoirs, a group of about a dozen pools, which include natural banks and some islands, on one of which is a heronry. Access is by permit only from Ferry Lane, a turning off the A503 which runs between Waltham-stow and Tottenham, or between the A10 and the A11.

Further up the Lea Valley, between Edmonton and Ponders End, lies the William Girling Reservoir (TQ 3794). The Ponders End to Chingford road crosses the valley and separates this reservoir from the King George V to the north. The latter is further divided by a causeway. Access is by permit only.

WILDFOWL (Walthamstow)

Mallard	100– 250
Shoveler	100– 250
Pochard	500–1000
Tufted Duck	500–1000

Also: Teal

WILDFOWL (William Girling)

Mallard	100–250
Teal	100–250
Shoveler	100–250
Tufted Duck	100–250
Goldeneye	<100
Goosander	<100

Also: Pochard

WILDFOWL (King George V)

Mallard	<100
Pochard	100–500
Tufted Duck	250–500
Goldeneye	<100
Goosander	<100

Queen Elizabeth II Reservoir   *Sheet 176 TQ 1267*

One of the newer reservoirs, the Queen Elizabeth lies near Walton-on-Thames and has been more attractive to dabbling ducks in recent years than other waters to the west of London. Access is by permit only, and is from the B369 (East Mosely to Walton) road.

WILDFOWL

Mallard	250–500
Teal	100–250
Shoveler	100–500
Tufted Duck	100–250

Also: Wigeon, Goldeneye

Queen Mary (Littleton) Reservoir   *Sheet 176 TQ 0770*

Lying just a couple of miles south-east of Staines Reservoir, the
Queen Mary, at 292 ha (707 acres), is one of the largest in the area.
Although there is sailing on it, it has been popular with the ducks in
recent years, as the figures below confirm. The reservoir lies adjacent
to the A308 (Staines to Sunbury) road and access is through the main
entrance at the eastern end down a side road off the A308.

WILDFOWL

Shoveler	100– 250
Pochard	100– 250
Tufted Duck	500–1000
Goldeneye	<100
Goosander	<100

Also: Mallard

Staines Reservoir   *Sheet 176 TQ 0573*

The King George VI and Staines reservoirs are divided by the A3044
which connects Staines with the A4. Staines Reservoir is further
divided by a causeway accessible from the B378, on the eastern side of
the reservoir, which runs between the A3044 and the A30. This gives
complete views over both halves of the reservoir.

WILDFOWL

Pochard	100–250
Tufted Duck	100–250
Goosander	<100

Also: Mallard, Teal, Wigeon, Shoveler, Goldeneye
Other birds: Black-necked Grebes

MANCHESTER (GREATER)

There are a number of small hill reservoirs to the north and east of the city of Manchester, but even taken together they do not hold more than small numbers of the commoner wildfowl.

MERSEYSIDE

As already mentioned under Cheshire, the Mersey estuary, which lies between that county and Merseyside, is inaccessible at the best bird site on the south side. The north bank can be reached through Garston, Speke and Hale but, alas, most of the ducks are on the far side of the estuary. At the north end of the county, it includes the sand off Southport, but the rest of the Ribble estuary, of which the sand forms the outermost part, lies in Lancashire and is dealt with there.

NORFOLK

The coast of Norfolk is rich in wetlands, with the north coast in particular virtually one continuum of good habitat, the greater part of it protected by reserves. The Norfolk shore of the Wash, too, is of high quality (this area is covered under Lincolnshire). On the east coast of the county, the enclosed estuary of Breydon Water is of considerable importance. Of the Broads, only Hickling and Horsey, lying close together near the coast, are of importance to wildfowl; the remainder are too disturbed. Elsewhere inland the county is relatively dry, with only the Breckland pools holding small numbers of the commoner species. The fenland part of Norfolk contains part of the Ouse Washes, which are covered under Cambridgeshire.

Breydon Water   *Sheet 134 TG 4907*

This tidal estuary lies immediately behind Great Yarmouth and has
only a narrow outlet to the sea, through the town. It covers about 760
ha (1,900 acres) with very extensive mudflats and some saltmarsh, and
it is surrounded by low-lying pasture land. Numbers of wildfowl and
waders are not great but there is considerable variety of species
including swans and geese. A small flock of Bean Geese, whose main
wintering area is at Buckenham on the River Yare, often come to
Breydon too, and there are small wintering flocks of White-fronted
Geese and Bewick's Swans.

A public footpath linking Great Yarmouth with Burgh Castle runs
along the southern shore of Breydon Water. In Great Yarmouth the
path starts from the north end of the town on the west bank of the
river. Approaching the town from the south on the A12 from
Lowestoft, go straight on when the road turns sharp right to cross the
river. Burgh Castle is reached down lanes from the A143 (Great
Yarmouth to Bungay) road, turning right soon after leaving Great
Yarmouth.

On the north side a lane leads from Freethorpe village on the B1140
(Acle to Reedham) to the Berney Arms Inn whence it is possible to
take a public footpath along the north bank of the estuary.

WILDFOWL

Mute Swan	100–250
Bewick's Swan	<100
Bean Goose	<100
White-fronted Goose	100–250
Shelduck	250–500
Mallard	<100
Teal	<100
Wigeon	250–500
Pintail	100–250
Scaup	<100
Goldeneye	<100

Also: Shoveler, Pochard, Tufted Duck

WADERS

Dunlin	2500–5000
Knot	250–500
Redshank	250–500

Also: Oystercatcher, Ringed Plover, Grey Plover, Sanderling, Bar-tailed
Godwit, Whimbrel
Other birds: raptors and passage terns

Hickling Pond and Horsey Mere   *Sheet 134 TG 4322*
The open water area of Hickling Pond is about 155 ha (380 acres), and
that of Horsey Mere about 34 ha (85 acres). Both are surrounded by
extensive reedbeds and fen which are the home of a wide variety of
breeding birds, including Bittern, Marsh and Montagu's Harriers,
Bearded Tit and Garganey. Wintering wildfowl are numerous.
particularly on the larger Hickling, although most species are also
present at Horsey.
 Both waters are reserves and at Hickling the Norfolk Naturalists'
Trust has built an information centre and public hides. These are
reached from the road leading to Hickling village from the A149
(Great Yarmouth to North Walsham). Horsey Mere is not so readily
visible but can be seen from the B1159 which runs through Horsey
village, particularly from the windmill about 0.8 km (½ mile) south of
the village, whence a public footpath leads round the north-east side.

WILDFOWL (both waters)

Mute Swan	<100
Whooper Swan	<100
Bewick's Swan	<100
Canada Goose	<100
Mallard	1000–2500
Teal	1000–2500
Wigeon	100– 500
Gadwall	100– 250
Shoveler	250– 500
Pochard	100– 250
Tufted Duck	100– 250
Goldeneye	<100

North Norfolk Coast   *Sheets 132 & 133 TF 9045*
Between Holme in the west and Salthouse, near Sheringham, the
north coast of Norfolk offers a mixture of saltmarsh, sand-dune,
mudflats, shingle banks and estuaries. The bird life of the area is very
rich with, in particular, large colonies of breeding terns, including

Sandwich, Common and Little, while the area around Cley has produced a steady stream of rare migrants. However, despite the concentration of bird-watchers that this brings to the area, there is a lack of systematic counts and no good series from which to construct meaningful tables of peak and regular numbers for either wildfowl or waders. The wintering Dark-bellied Brent have been counted in most years, with peaks of up to 6,000, while Shelduck, Mallard, Teal and Wigeon all occur in substantial numbers. Sea ducks occur offshore, and at Hunstanton, just inside the Wash, there are flocks of up to 2,000 Common Scoter, plus small numbers of Velvet Scoter and Eider. Wader numbers, too, are thought to be large, though there is quite a lot of movement in and out of the Wash, especially of birds flying round the Hunstanton corner to roost at Holme. Knot do this regularly.

The A149 (Hunstanton to Sheringham) runs along the north coast. Going from west to east, one starts in Hunstanton where the sea duck flocks are often visible from the clifftop at the north end of the town. The next area is Holme and Thornham Harbour. Holme Beach is signposted off the A140, as is a private nature reserve and bird observatory. Thornham Harbour is reached down a track to the seawall from Thornham village. Next comes Scolt Head Island and the extensive saltmarshes and tidal channels between the island and the coast road. The island is a National Nature Reserve but there is access by boat or walking at low tide, though not to the area where the terns are breeding in the summer. The starting point is Brancaster Staithe, and it is also possible to walk along the seawalls running in either direction, to obtain views over the mudflats and marsh. This is true, too, at Overy Staithe, the next village along the A149.

There follows a drier stretch, with pine-covered sand-dunes along the shore, broken at Wells by a tidal inlet running back to the town. The A149 bypasses Wells on the south side, so head for the town centre and then drive down the east side of the inlet to a car park near the lifeboat station at the mouth.

The last area is that of Blakeney Point and Cley Marshes. Blakeney is a long shingle arm stretching to the east and enclosing a wide area of saltmarsh and mudflats, much favoured by wildfowl and waders. The Morston saltmarshes can be traversed on foot starting from either Morston or Blakeney, both lying on the A149, while the point is reached from the village of Cley or by boat from Morston in the summer.

The stretch of coast between Cley and Salthouse contains

freshwater marsh, pools and reedbeds, and has a good list of wintering and passage waders and wildfowl as well as many breeding birds. The Norfolk Naturalists' Trust owns most of the area and there are hides overlooking the reserve. Permits can be obtained from the Trust at 4 The Close, Norwich, or from the warden at Cley.

NORTHAMPTONSHIRE _

To the north of Northampton lie three reservoirs of some importance; Pitsford, Hollowell and Ravensthorpe. The first of these is the best, and at peak can hold several hundred each of Mallard, Teal, Wigeon, Pochard and Tufted Duck. It is used for sailing but, being split in two by a causeway, disturbance is reduced sufficiently to allow the ducks necessary sanctuary. Hollowell and Ravensthorpe lie close together and also hold useful numbers of the five common species. Elsewhere the county is comparatively dry, with just a few small lakes and impoundments.

NORTHUMBERLAND ___

There is one very important coastal wetland in this county—the Lindisfarne National Nature Reserve, covering the large area of flats between the mainland and Holy Island. Elsewhere the coast is unsuitable for waterfowl, apart from the small numbers found at the mouths of some of the lesser rivers. Sea ducks are quite plentiful along the coast and can be seen to advantage at, for example, Seaton Sluice near Whitby. The Tweed estuary is not particularly good, though small numbers of waders occur. Inland in Northumberland are a number of lowland pools which attract a good variety of birds, if not in very large numbers. These pools include Cresswell ponds near Ashington; and the Holywell ponds not far from Seaton Sluice. Further inland there are the Whittledene reservoirs, lying astride Hadrian's Wall, the B6318, about 19 km (12 miles) west of

Newcastle. These carry a few hundred diving ducks in the winter, plus occasional Smew and Goosander. Another 32 km (20 miles) along the same road brings one to Greenlee and Broomlee Loughs, which hold small numbers of duck, while north from Corbridge up the A68 are Colt Crag and Hallington Reservoirs, where Whooper Swans and some duck occur.

Lindisfarne National Nature Reserve   *Sheet 75 NU 1042*

The reserve covers a total of 3,650 ha (9,000 acres) of which nearly 3,200 ha (8,000 acres) are mudflats, plus about 40 ha (100 acres) of saltmarsh. There are both *Zostera* and *Enteromorpha* on the flats and these attract enormous numbers of Wigeon, making it the most important coastal site for this species in the country; also the largest flock of Light-bellied Brent Geese outside Ireland. These birds belong to the Svalbard population which mainly winters in Denmark. Depending on the weather on the other side of the North Sea, numbers coming across the sea vary from a few hundred to over 1,500. At the peak this may represent two-thirds or more of this tiny population. The entire area is a National Nature Reserve but permits are not required for access to the shore or across the tidal causeway to Holy Island. The much smaller Budle Bay, to the south, is also included in the Reserve and in the following counts.

The main A1 (between Alnwick and Berwick-on-Tweed) passes within a few miles of the flats and there are several points of access down lanes from that road. The lane through Beal leads onto Holy Island itself with views back across the flats or, from the island, out to sea where sea ducks are often present. South from there one can reach the flats through Fenham, turning off the A1 at Fenwick, at Fenham Lowmoor, or through Elwick or Ross. Budle Bay is best observed from the south going through Warren Mill to Budle.

WILDFOWL

Whooper Swan	100– 250
Greylag Goose	500–1000
Brent Goose	500–1000
Shelduck	500–1000
Mallard	500–1000
Teal	250– 500
Wigeon	10000+
Eider	1000–2500

Common Scoter	500–1000
Long-tailed Duck	100– 250
Red-breasted Merganser	<100

Also: Mute Swan, Pintail, Pochard, Tufted Duck, Scaup, Goldeneye

WADERS

Oystercatcher	1000– 2500
Ringed Plover	100– 250
Golden Plover	1000– 2500
Grey Plover	100– 250
Lapwing	1000– 2500
Turnstone	100– 250
Dunlin	10000+
Knot	5000–10000
Sanderling	100– 250
Redshank	1000– 2500
Bar-tailed Godwit	2500– 5000
Curlew	500– 1000

Also: Purple Sandpiper, Ruff, Spotted Redshank, Greenshank
Other birds: divers and grebes
The Wigeon flock is one of the largest in the country

NOTTINGHAMSHIRE ___

Scattered along the Trent valley in the south and east of the county are several groups of gravel pits, such as those at Attenborough, Radcliffe, Gunthorpe, Hoveringham, South Muskham and Besthorpe. At Attenborough there is a county trust reserve which has helped both dabbling and diving ducks reach several hundred at peak, while there is also a sizeable population of Canada Geese using several of the groups of pits.

In the centre and west of the county, the Dukeries, there are several park lakes of varying value, but those at Welbeck, Thoresby, Clumber and Carburton do attract Mallard and Teal as well as diving ducks. Both Goldeneye and Goosander are regular in winter.

OXFORDSHIRE _____

The Thames valley, running through the county, has extensive gravel deposits which have been worked in a number of localities. There are good pits at Standlake, west of Oxford, Dorchester and Sutton Courtenay to the south, and at Sonning, in the very south of the county near Reading. Near the Standlake pits is Farmoor reservoir which, when not being sailed on, carries useful numbers of several duck species.

Floods along the Cherwell valley near Aynho can be good when not disturbed, with Bewick's Swan regular. However, they are threatened with further drainage and the passage of a new road.

SHROPSHIRE _____

The only significant waters in this large county are two groups of meres in the north. The first group is centred round Ellesmere, which is also the name of the largest pool. Along with Colemere, Whitemere and a few smaller pools, it holds some hundreds of Mallard, Wigeon and Tufted Duck, as well as regular Teal, Pintail, Shoveler, Pochard, Goldeneye and Goosander. A large flock of Canada Geese is also present. The second group is a few miles to the east, round the town of Whitchurch. The principal waters are Combermere, Barmere, Shavington Hall and Marbury. Together they hold very similar numbers of the same species as at Ellesmere, though with even more Canada Geese.

SOMERSET _____

The old county of Somerset contained three fine reservoirs, but has lost two—Chew and Blagdon—to Avon, keeping only Cheddar. On the coast the National Nature Reserve of Bridgwater Bay is a particularly good area, with few other coastal sites of great interest, though Sand Bay to the north holds some waders. The Somerset Levels, low-lying pasture flooded in winter, still carry sizeable flocks of ducks and swans, although they are much drained and disturbed and are threatened with more to come.

Bridgwater Bay National Nature Reserve   *Sheet 182 ST 2847*

Situated on the south side of the Bristol Channel where the coastline makes a right-angled turn from north–south to east–west, this great shallow bay includes over 3,880 ha (8,000 acres) of mud and sandflats, rich in invertebrates; 150 ha (370 acres) of marsh; and about 120 ha (295 acres) of shingle. Two small islands off Steart Point provide roosts for very large numbers of waders. In late summer the sandflats are the moulting ground for up to 3,000 Shelduck and are one of the very few areas away from the Heligoland Bight in the south-eastern North Sea where the adults of this species moult. Of the other ducks, Wigeon is easily the most important. White-fronted Geese formerly roosted on the Bay, flighting inland to feed, but virtually none have been seen for over 15 years. A feature of the waders is an April–May build-up of Whimbrel to form the largest flock in the country.

The best view over the bay is from the west side of the Parrett estuary. Take the A39 (Bridgwater to Minehead) and turn north at Cannington, going through Combwich to Steart village. A footpath leads on from here to Steart Point where the Nature Conservancy have recently excavated a scrape just inside the point and erected a hide. On the east side of the Parrett it is possible to overlook the point from the coast south of Burnham-on-Sea by walking out to the beach from Huntspill on the A38 (Bridgwater to Weston).

WILDFOWL

Shelduck (moulting)	1000–2500
Shelduck (winter)	1000–2500
Mallard	1000–2500
Teal	250– 500
Wigeon	1000–2500
Pintail	<100
Shoveler	<100

WADERS

Oystercatcher	100– 250
Lapwing	500–1000
Dunlin	1000–2500
Redshank	500–1000
Black-tailed Godwit	500–1000
Curlew	100– 250
Whimbrel	500–1000

Also: Grey Plover, Turnstone, Knot, Bar-tailed Godwit
Easily the largest flock of Whimbrel in Britain, up to 5% of the total

Cheddar Reservoir *Sheet 182 ST 4454*

This completely artificial reservoir, nearly circular and with concrete banks, attracts surprising numbers of wildfowl. Sailing on certain days of the week drives many of the birds away, often over the Mendips to Chew and Blagdon, and there are perhaps fewer ducks than there used to be. The diversity is, however, still considerable.

The reservoir is owned by the same Bristol Waterworks as Chew and Blagdon (Avon), and a permit giving access to the reservoir itself is needed from them and can be obtained by applying to Woodford Lodge at Chew Stoke. The entrance to the reservoir is on the northern side, reached from the village of Axbridge just west of Cheddar.

WILDFOWL

Mallard	250– 500
Teal	500–1000
Gadwall	<100
Wigeon	100– 500
Shoveler	<100
Pochard	500–1000
Tufted Duck	100– 250

Also: Mute Swan, Pintail, Goldeneye

Somerset Levels *Sheet 182*

It is difficult to provide good information either for numbers of birds or the localities in which to find them in this area, as both are wholly dependent on flood conditions. There are a number of areas where flooding occurs but the use made of them by wildfowl will be dictated by the depth and duration of the water, the amount of disturbance, and so on. Most of the dabbling ducks can be found, with Teal and Wigeon in the largest numbers (up to 1,000 or more), while a winter flock of 100–300 Bewick's Swans has been present in most recent winters.

The three best areas for floods and for ducks and swans are: Wetmoor (ST 4525), south of Langport, between the villages of Muchelney and Long Load; West Sedge Moor (ST 3526), in the area between Curry Rivel, Burrow Bridge, Durston and North Curry; and Tealham Moor (ST 4046), much further north, south-west of Wedmore.

STAFFORDSHIRE ───────

The county of Staffordshire has little water: there are some gravel pits, private lakes and small reservoirs, but their importance to waterfowl is small. Of the larger waters, Belvide reservoir and Gailey Pools, beside the A5 north of Wolverhampton, both carry useful numbers of the commoner ducks, but the only significant water is Blithfield reservoir near Rugeley.

Blithfield Reservoir *Sheet 128 SK 0624*
The reservoir covers about 325 ha (800 acres) and is divided into two parts by a central causeway, the B5013. Although there is sailing on the lower half, and fishing on both, the winter disturbance to the upper part is small and the wildfowl appreciate this. Two streams feed the reservoir and marshy ground extends along both from the water's edge.

The B5013 which crosses the causeway leaves Rugeley going north towards Abbots Bromley. Small lanes lead off round the head of the reservoir through Newton and give some views of the upper half, while on the east bank a lane leads south just past the causeway for a view of the lower part.

WILDFOWL

Canada Goose	100– 250
Mallard	1000–2500
Teal	500–1000
Wigeon	500–1000
Pochard	250– 500
Tufted Duck	100– 250
Goldeneye	<100
Goosander	<100

Also: Bewick's Swan, Mute Swan, Shoveler (100–250)
Other birds: grebes, passage waders and terns

SUFFOLK _____

Compared with Essex lying just to the south, Suffolk is nothing like
so well off for wetlands. At the southern end of the coast there are
the Orwell and Deben estuaries, both rather narrow and much
disturbed by sailing, without the very extensive mudflats which
characterize the Essex estuaries and which both provide wildfowl
and wader habitat and restrict recreational activities. Small numbers
of typical species occur in both estuaries.

Going north, one comes to the very complex channels of the Alde,
Ore and Butley Creek. These channels surround Havergate Island,
the famous breeding site of the Avocet and a reserve of the RSPB.
Very large numbers of ducks, especially Mallard, Teal and Wigeon,
formerly wintered here, but they have decreased sharply in recent
years and now rarely reach 1,000 each. The main part of the estuary
lies behind the town of Aldeburgh and can be viewed best from the
south side by walking from the village of Iken.

Further north one reaches the complex of marshes and pools
embraced by the nearly adjacent Minsmere Reserve of the RSPB and
the Walberswick National Nature Reserve, separated from the short
cliff stretch round Dunwich. These are dealt with below.

Inland Suffolk is comparatively dry, though the Breckland pools overlapping the border into Norfolk hold useful numbers of the commoner ducks and also Canada Geese.

Minsmere and Walberswick   *Sheet 156 TM 4767 and 4773*
The Minsmere Reserve of the RSPB covers about 850 ha (2,100 acres) and the Walberswick National Nature Reserve about 1,050 ha (2,600 acres). They both include mudflats, pools, reedbeds, heathland and shingle banks. While more noted for their enormous variety of breeding birds, substantial numbers of wildfowl also winter, particularly on Minsmere with its specially created open water 'scrapes'.

Access to the Minsmere Reserve is by permit only, obtainable in advance from the Permit Secretary, Minsmere Reserve, Westleton, Saxmundham, Suffolk for a small fee. There is, however, free access to public hides on the coastal shingle strip reached by driving and then walking south from the village of Dunwich, midway between Southwold and Aldeburgh.

Walberswick NNR contains several public footpaths, reached either from the village of Walberswick, just south of Southwold, or north from Dunwich. Some of the paths follow old raised walls which give useful visibility over the great reedbeds.

WILDFOWL

Mute Swan	<100
Bewick's Swan	<100
Canada Goose	100– 250
Shelduck	<100
Mallard	250– 500
Teal	500–1000
Wigeon	250– 500
Shoveler	100– 250
Gadwall	100– 250

Other birds: passage waders and terns, migrants

SURREY ⎯⎯⎯⎯⎯⎯⎯⎯⎯⎯⎯⎯

Essentially a dry, rather hilly county, Surrey has few waters, and those are mostly small and not important for wildfowl. Frensham Ponds, near Farnham, hold useful numbers of Tufted Duck, and some fairly recently excavated gravel pits between Guildford and Woking are becoming quite attractive.

SUSSEX ⎯⎯⎯⎯⎯⎯⎯⎯⎯⎯⎯⎯

Like Hampshire, Sussex has its wetland riches on the coast in the form of shallow harbours with extensive low-tide flats. The westernmost, Chichester harbour, is in fact partly in Hampshire and is connected with Langstone harbour round the northern end of Hayling Island. However it gets its name from a prominent Sussex town and is usually regarded as within this county. Not far away is the much smaller Pagham harbour, while at the extreme eastern end of the county, past chalk cliffs, caravan sites and several holiday towns, is Rye harbour.

Inland there is little water, though extensive gravel pits close to Rye harbour, and south-east of the town of Chichester, are quite attractive to wildfowl. Winter flooding of the Arun River at Pulborough and at Amberley was formerly regular and considerable, but recent drainage has meant a lessening of floods, and schemes are planned that could prevent them altogether, though these are being resisted. Wigeon and Teal were very numerous here 15 years ago or more but only a few hundreds have occurred in recent years.

Several small lakes and reservoirs are scattered through Sussex, as at Duncton, Arlington, Darwell and Weirwood, but numbers of duck at all are comparatively small, with Weirwood perhaps the best and Mallard, Pochard and Tufted Duck all reaching the low hundreds.

Chichester Harbour   *Sheet 197 SU 7601*
As already mentioned, this harbour is connected by a tidal channel

with Langstone harbour. It is much the larger of the two with a total area of about 2,400 ha (5,900 acres), of which roughly two-thirds is tidal flats, mainly rich clay-silt with large areas of *Zostera* and *Enteromorpha* and notably diverse and abundant invertebrate life. Thorney Deep is the single most important area for wildfowl, while the most important wader roost is Pitsey Island. The remaining third is saltmarsh, plus a small amount of shingle on which terns breed. Chichester harbour has four long arms stretching back inland, and the two eastern ones in particular have become major yacht anchorages and so of reduced value to birds.

As in neighbouring Langstone harbour, the outstanding birds are Dark-bellied Brent Geese and Dunlin among the wildfowl and waders respectively. It is not clear how much interchange there is between the two harbours, but the counts have been co-ordinated to produce realistic figures for each.

Views over the western part of the harbour can be obtained from Hayling Island, which is reached by a turning off the A27 south coast trunk road at Havant, as described under Langstone harbour, Hampshire (p. 93). Two other turnings off the A27 further east lead to West Thorney, on Thorney Island, round which a public footpath runs along the coast, and to Chidham, from both of which quite good views can be had. Perhaps the best area is the east side, approached from Chichester along the A286 to West Wittering. At the latter place one can walk to the point at East Head, or go further to West Itchenor, whence again it is possible to walk westwards along the coast on a public footpath.

WILDFOWL

Brent Goose	5000–10000
Shelduck	2500– 5000
Mallard	100– 250
Teal	250– 500
Wigeon	500– 1000
Pintail	100– 250

Also: Mute Swan (100–250), Pochard (100–250), Goldeneye (100–250), Eider, Red-breasted Merganser

WADERS

Oystercatcher	500–1000
Ringed Plover	100– 250

Grey Plover	500–1000
Lapwing	1000–2500
Turnstone	100– 250
Dunlin	20000+
Knot	250– 500
Sanderling	250– 500
Redshank	1000–2500
Black-tailed Godwit	500–1000
Bar-tailed Godwit	500–1000

Also: Golden Plover (250–500), Greenshank
Other birds: divers and grebes, particularly Black-necked and Slavonian

Pagham Harbour   *Sheet 197 SZ 8796*
Although the comparatively small size of Pagham harbour—it is just 240 ha (600 acres)—precludes really large numbers of birds, there is the advantage that distances are fairly small and good views are therefore usually possible. Adjacent pools at Sidlesham, and the permanent water area of Pagham Lagoon, add to the attractiveness of the place, particularly during migration.

It is possible to walk round virtually the whole shore of the harbour, the main access points being at Sidlesham, Church Norton and Pagham. For the first two, leave Chichester on the B2145 road to Selsey: Sidlesham is on that road, which also passes by Sidlesham Ferry and its pools. A right turn shortly after there takes one to Church Norton and the southern side of the mouth. Pagham is reached by turning off the B2145 on to the B2166 (Aldwick and Bognor) road, then right. Turning right in Pagham brings one to the edge of the harbour.

WILDFOWL

Brent Goose	100– 250
Shelduck	500–1000
Mallard	100– 250
Teal	100– 250
Pintail	<100

Also: Shoveler, Eider, Red-breasted Merganser

WADERS

Oystercatcher	100– 250
Ringed Plover	100– 250
Grey Plover	100– 250
Turnstone	100– 250
Dunlin	2500–5000
Redshank	250– 500
Black-tailed Godwit	100– 250

Also: Lapwing (100–500), Bar-tailed Godwit

Rye Harbour *Sheet 189 TQ 9419*

Although the harbour at Rye is quite small, the extensive gravel pits alongside and the sheltered Rye Bay combine to form an important waterfowl resort. Sea ducks—in particular Common Scoter—have been noted in some thousands, but in recent years they seem to have decreased to a few hundred. The growth of the gravel pits, however, has allowed diving ducks to winter in the area in some numbers.

The area is reached from the A259 (Rye to Hastings) by turning right off it a short distance out of Rye to Rye harbour. Tracks and paths lead to the pits and to the harbour mouth. Some of the pits are included in an RSPB reserve to which entrance is by permit, allowing access to hides overlooking some of the pits, in particular those with breeding terns.

WILDFOWL

Mallard	250–500
Teal	<100
Wigeon	<100
Pochard	250–500
Tufted Duck	100–250
Common Scoter	100–250

Also: Mute Swan, Gadwall, Shoveler, Smew

WADERS

Oystercatcher	250– 500
Lapwing	500–1000
Dunlin	100– 250

| Sanderling | <100 |
| Redshank | <100 |

Also: Ringed Plover (100–250), Grey Plover, Turnstone, Bar-tailed Godwit

TYNE AND WEAR————

This largely urban county has no important wetlands, with just the lake at Gosforth Park, on the northern side of Newcastle, providing at least one locality where ducks can live. It has long been maintained as a sanctuary by the county trust and several hundred ducks of a variety of species occur there.

WARWICKSHIRE————

This central England county has only a very few waters within its boundaries and most of these are either too small or too disturbed to be of great value to ducks. Alvecote pools, in the very north of the county near Tamworth, is probably the most attractive water. It is a reserve of the West Midland Trust for Nature Conservation and carries a good variety of duck as well as passage waders and terns. Draycote Water, just south of Rugby, is too disturbed by sailing to fulfil the potential which its size suggests, but it none the less attracts quite good numbers of duck.

WEST MIDLANDS _____

There are a few lakes and small reservoirs within this predominantly urban county but there is little of interest to wildfowl, apart from some Canada Geese on some sites.

WILTSHIRE _____

There is very little standing water in Wiltshire—the combination of limestone in the west and chalk elsewhere sees to that. In the extreme north-west corner of the county, the extensive gravel pits of the Cotswold Water Park extend just over the border from Gloucestershire, but have been dealt with in detail under that county (p. 88). Coate Water on the edge of Swindon is now rather disturbed as a public park but a hide has been erected at the southern end and the sailing restricted in order to allow the birds some sanctuary, though numbers are small. Otherwise there are just a few lakes in private parks, such as Corsham, Longleat and Fonthill, holding a few of the commoner species.

YORKSHIRE (NORTH) _____

In its former existence, the county of Yorkshire, despite being the largest in England, was short on really important wetlands, and now that the Humber has been lost to Humberside, its new component parts of North, West and South Yorkshire lack any coastal wetlands at all and are also short on inland ones. Although there are a great many reservoirs within the three counties, most are too small, or too high up, to attract really good numbers of duck. Only Gouthwaite reservoir in Nidderdale carries an interesting variety, if not numbers, of duck, together with waders when there is mud exposed.

The sole remaining wetland of real importance is the floodland of the River Derwent, between Bubwith and Wheldrake. It is now actually on the border with Humberside and, indeed, is best approached from that, the eastern side. However, as part of the area is a reserve of the Yorkshire Naturalists' Trust, it seemed best to include it in North Yorkshire and thus to give that county some representation in this book.

Derwent Floods, Bubwith to Wheldrake   *Sheet 106 SE 7044*

The River Derwent meanders slowly on its way through the eastern Yorkshire plain and once had an extensive flood area on either side. Drainage and straightening have removed much of this until now only the stretch between Bubwith and Wheldrake, to the north-east of Selby, floods with any regularity. Even here, as with any riverside floods, the threat of improved drainage must hang over the future.

When the floods are out the duck quickly assemble and numbers—in particular of Bewick's Swans and Wigeon—can be high. The reserve established over part of the area has helped to cut down disturbance. The floods can be seen from a number of vantage points reached from the B1228 (Bubwith to York). This is a turning off the A163 (Welby to Market Weighton) about 9 miles east of Selby. From the B1228 take side roads to the villages of Aughton, Ellerton, East Cottingwith and Storwood.

WILDFOWL

Bewick's Swan	100– 250
Mallard	250– 500
Teal	500–1000
Wigeon	1000–5000
Pochard	100– 500

Also: Whooper Swan, Pintail, Tufted Duck

YORKSHIRE (SOUTH) _____

The hills of South Yorkshire contain many reservoirs but all are on acid soil and contain little food for birds. Those waters on lower ground are too small or too disturbed to hold more than a handful of ducks.

YORKSHIRE (WEST) _____

There are a large number of hill reservoirs in the west of this county in the hills of the southern Pennines, but they are virtually all strongly oligotrophic and support few birds. Eccup reservoir and nearby Harewood Park Lake carry a large flock of Canada Geese, and several hundred Mallard, plus small numbers of a few other species. Some mining subsidences and associated winter flooding near Castleford have proved quite attractive, especially at Fairburn where the declaration of a local nature reserve has helped considerably.

WALES _____

CLWYD

The major wetland of the Dee estuary has been dealt with under Cheshire (p. 55), in which county it also lies. Elsewhere in Clwyd there is little of interest to wildfowl.

DYFED

This very large county covers most of the southern half of west Wales. Inland wetlands are not important, being mostly oligotrophic hill lakes and reservoirs. There is one important inland haunt of White-fronted Geese, in the Towy Valley between Llandeilo and Carmarthen, which has gained in importance in recent years while other haunts have been declining. Several hundred Wigeon and large flocks of Golden Plover add to the interest of the area, which is dealt with below. On the coast the three estuaries of the Gwendraeth, Towy and Taf form a complex of sand and mudflats round Carmarthen Bay but hold relatively few birds considering their size. It is probable that feeding conditions are not very good and there is considerable disturbance from military activity. Out in Carmarthen Bay there are flocks of Common Scoter throughout much of the year, with both wintering and moulting (summer) peaks, but the birds can not easily be seen from land.

Going round the coast westwards, the multiple arms of Milford Haven which reach a long way back inland hold small numbers of typical ducks and waders, but there is no single site of great importance. Perhaps the best area is along the Western Cleddau around Fowborough and Little Milford, reached by walking the river bank eastwards from Hook, not far south of Haverfordwest. From Milford Haven northwards the coast is rocky and largely inhospitable all the way up past Aberystwyth until one reaches Dyfi estuary on the border with Gwynedd. This is probably the best wetland in western Wales for wildfowl and waders.

Inland the northern half of Dyfed is lacking any good wetlands for birds. There was formerly a wintering flock of Greenland White-fronted Geese at Cors Tregaron, but they left the area in the early

1960s and have not returned on a regular basis. What is probably the remnant of this flock now winters on the Dyfi estuary.

Dyfi Estuary   *Sheet 135 SN 6495*
This estuary covers about 2,000 ha (4,950 acres) in all, of which about three-quarters are sandflats with some silt. The remaining quarter is saltmarsh which extends in a belt along the south shore, with more extensive areas near the mouth and at the head of the estuary. There are good numbers of ducks in the estuary, especially Mallard, Teal, Wigeon and Pintail; while, although waders are not numerous, there is a good variety.

A small, and decreasing, flock of Greenland Whitefronts roosts on the estuary sands and feeds mainly in Borth Bog, a relatively inaccessible area to the south of the estuary. Until the 1960s it was always thought that this flock was of European Whitefronts—and indeed this may have been so—but certainly in the last 12 years, at least, only Greenland Whitefronts have occurred here. It is possibly the same flock, now much reduced, that formerly wintered at Tregaron Bog, not far away. Despite attempts to regulate shooting on the estuary with the creation of a sizeable reserve, it seems that this and the associated disturbance have contributed to the decline in the flock which has dropped from 100–200 in the late 1960s to the present level.

The A493 (Aberdyfi to Machynlleth) runs along the northern shore of the estuary, giving excellent views at a number of points. From the south side observation is more difficult, although it is possible to walk along the railway line which runs close to the shore in places, joining it either near the mouth close to Ynyslas or at the head of the estuary at Glandyfi. The RSPB has a reserve at Ynyshir to which access is by permit (obtained from RSPB Welsh Office, 18 High Street, Newton, Powys). This covers an area at the very head of the estuary and small numbers of many waterfowl species are found there.

WILDFOWL

White-fronted Goose	<100
Shelduck	100– 250
Mallard	500–1000
Teal	500–1000

Wigeon	1000–2500
Pintail	250– 500
Red-breasted	
Merganser	<100

Also: Shoveler, Goldeneye

WADERS

Oystercatcher	500–1000
Ringed Plover	500–1000
Lapwing	250– 500
Dunlin	1000–2500
Sanderling	100– 250
Redshank	100– 250
Curlew	250– 500

Also: Grey Plover, Knot, Bar-tailed Godwit, Whimbrel

Towy Valley (near Carmarthen)   *Sheet 159 SN 5520*

The River Towy meanders its way along the 24 km (15 miles) from Llandeilo to Carmarthen bordered by low-lying flood-meadows which in certain stretches provide feeding ground for European White-fronted Geese, Wigeon and Golden Plover. The flock of Whitefronts is usually the second largest in the country after that at the New Grounds in Gloucestershire which lies about 120 km (75 miles) due east. It has increased in recent years, thanks to protection from the landowner, at a time when other sites, particularly in north Wales near Montgomery, have declined almost to extinction. Bird-watchers in this valley are urged not to disturb the geese if at all possible as they are very sensitive to disturbance. The Wigeon can usually be found feeding in the same area as the Whitefronts, sharing the latter's fondness for short grass. The Golden Plover, which can number up to 4,000—making it one of the largest flocks in the country—may range further afield.

This stretch of the Towy valley is bounded on the north by the main A40, and on the south by the B4300, which is a right turn off the A476 (Llandeilo to Llanelli) just south of Llandeilo. The B4300 gives the best views, particularly between Golden Grove and the right turn leading to Dryslwyn Castle. The Whitefronts are most often to be found between these two points, unless they have been badly disturbed, though they can also be found feeding west of Dryslwyn. If they cannot be seen from the B4300 it is worth going down the lane between Golden Grove and Llangathen, or the one leading to

Dryslwyn village. There is also a disused railway line along which it is possible to walk, although a demolished bridge prevents one going the full length of it.

One final area worth looking at is the pools near Nantgaredig, further west from Dryslwyn, which carry dabbling ducks and occasional Bewick's Swans.

WILDFOWL

White-fronted Goose	500–1000
Mallard	100– 500
Teal	100– 250
Wigeon	500–1000

GLAMORGAN ⸻

The old county of Glamorgan has been split into three and the one important wetland of the area, the Burry Inlet, is in fact in West Glamorgan and is shared with Dyfed. Elsewhere the coast has rather little to offer in the way of wetlands, while inland only a small number of artificial waters offer refuge to ducks. Of these, the industrial reservoir of Eglwys Nunydd beside the Margam steel-works holds useful numbers of diving ducks and some other species, as does Llanishen reservoir in north Cardiff.

Burry Inlet *Sheet 159 SS 9750*

The inlet is really the very broad estuary of the River Loughor. It is about 5,000 ha (12,350 acres) of which about two-thirds is sandflats and the remainder saltmarsh, including high marsh grazed by sheep. Near the mouth on the south side is a very large dune system which has been declared a National Nature Reserve.

The Burry is probably best known for the large flocks of Oystercatchers which have come into conflict with the cocklefishers of the area. Other waders, too, are numerous, while among the ducks, Wigeon, Pintail and Shelduck are most common. Small numbers of Dark-bellied Brent Geese winter here, the most westerly haunt of this race in Britain, and have been increasing recently in line with the national figures.

The best observation of the Burry is from the south side. Coming from the east take the A45/M4 Swansea bypass, then the A484 for Llanelli. Turn left at Gorseinon on the B4296 for Gowerton, then right on to the B4295. A Penclawdd the road reaches the shore giving excellent views over the upper estuary. Further along at Llanrhidian continue on unclassified roads for Cheriton. Just before the village a lane leads down to the shore at Llandimore, while through Cheriton to the end of the road a track and footpath take one along the east side of the Whiteford Burrows, giving good views over the outer estuary.

WILDFOWL

Brent Goose	<100
Shelduck	250– 500
Mallard	100– 250
Teal	250– 500
Wigeon	1000–2500
Pintail	250– 500

Also: Shoveler, Scaup, Eider, Red-breasted Merganser

WADERS

Oystercatcher	10000+
Ringed Plover	100– 250
Golden Plover	500– 1000
Grey Plover	100– 500
Lapwing	1000– 2500
Turnstone	500– 1000
Dunlin	5000–10000
Knot	5000–10000
Sanderling	100– 250
Redshank	1000– 2500
Black-tailed Godwit	100– 250
Bar-tailed Godwit	250– 500
Curlew	1000– 2500

Also: Purple Sandpiper, Spotted Redshank, Greenshank, Whimbrel

GWENT ──────────────

Gwent (formerly Monmouth) has a coastline on the lower Severn estuary but the shore is only moderately good for waders, the best stretch being the mouth of the Usk and north along the Caldicot Level. The latter area also holds some ducks, including Shelduck and Wigeon. The sizeable Llandegfedd Reservoir, just east of Pontypool, began promisingly while it was being filled but there is now regular sailing which prevents its being used to the full by wildfowl.

GWYNEDD ──────────────

There is just one wetland of importance in this new county which comprises the former Caernarvon, Merioneth, Montgomery and Anglesey—the estuary of Traeth Bach. The Dyfi estuary on the border with Dyfed has been dealt with under that county. Elsewhere estuaries are small and relatively unimportant and most inland waters are very oligotrophic. On Anglesey there are some more attractive waters, especially Llyn Coron and Malltraeth Bay, each holding up to 1,000 Wigeon, as well as several hundred Mallard.

Traeth Bach   *Sheet 124 SH 5736*
The River Dwyryd forms the estuary of Traeth Bach. The adjoining Traeth Mawr was formerly larger (hence its name) but has long since been reclaimed and only a small area of mudflats remains together with a more permanent pool near Portmadoc. The mudflats of both arms of the estuary total about 380 ha (940 acres), while there is an equal area of saltmarsh.

The numbers of wildfowl and waders are not large but of good variety and certainly of regional importance. Some sea ducks occur in the estuary though their status is not properly known.

The A496 (Barmouth to Ffestiniog) runs up the southern side of the estuary, and the A497 (Ffestiniog to Portmadoc) along the north. The Glaslyn Pool and the remains of Traeth Mawr can readily be seen from the A497 as it crosses the causeway just east of Portmadoc. On the south side make for the village of Llanfihangel-y-treathau, which lies on the A496, then, coming from Ffestiniog, turn right where the road turns sharp left into the village. Follow this road to the shore and walk west, or cross the creek to the east before reaching the shore and walk along the seawall.

WILDFOWL

Shelduck	100– 250
Mallard	250– 500
Teal	100– 250
Wigeon	500–1000
Pintail	100– 250
Shoveler	<100
Goldeneye	<100
Red-breasted Merganser	<100

Also: Whooper Swan, Mute Swan, Scaup, Eider

WADERS

Oystercatcher	500–1000
Lapwing	250– 500
Dunlin	250– 500
Redshank	100– 250
Curlew	250– 500

Also: Ringed Plover, Knot, Bar-tailed Godwit

POWYS

The various hill reservoirs of this county are not sufficiently productive to support wildfowl. Twenty years ago there was a large wintering flock of White-fronted Geese along the River Severn between Montgomery and Welshpool but changes in farming practices, improved drainage, and disturbance have driven them away and now a mere handful of birds appear. The steady decline of the goose flock was more or less paralleled by the increase in the flock in the Towy valley, Dyfed, so that Wales did not lose its Whitefronts altogether.

SCOTLAND

BORDERS

The south-east of Scotland is not well-off for good wetlands. The coast is relatively short and largely rocky. There are small numbers of birds at the mouth of the Tweed and some sea ducks along the coast to the north, but they are not significant. Inland there are some lakes and reservoirs holding small numbers of ducks, but the only ones of real value to waterfowl are in the extreme north of the county of Peebles—the reservoirs of Baddinsgill, Westwater and Portmore—which all act as roosts for varying numbers of Pink-footed Geese.

CENTRAL

The River Forth runs through this region, which also includes the upper part of its estuary or firth. The latter area is dealt with in detail under the Lothians which contains most of the remaining good bird areas of the firth. Inland the Forth meanders through a flat plain between Aberfoyle and Stirling. Both Greylags and Pinkfeet are found here feeding on the rich farmland, the Pinkfeet particularly near Thornhill and Kippen, while the Greylags are further west near their roosting site of the Lake of Menteith. The latter water also carries some duck. A flock of Whooper Swans is quite often to be found in the eastern part of the area. The Pinkfeet roost either on the pools in the centre of Flanders Moss or on hill lochs to the north. Just north of Alloa is Gartmorn Dam, a reservoir of about 57 ha (140 acres), which holds several hundred ducks, especially Mallard and Tufted Duck.

DUMFRIES
AND GALLOWAY ⸺

This region comprises the old counties of Dumfriesshire, Kirkcud-
brightshire and Wigtownshire. Much of the hinterland is comparatively dry and what lochs and reservoirs there are tend to be rather
oligotrophic. A major exception is Loch Ken, running north and east
from Castle Douglas. Here the water is comparatively fertile and the
loch attracts a wide variety of breeding and wintering wildfowl. The
area is also noted for its wintering flock of Bean, one of only two in
the country, together with Greenland White-fronted and Greylag
Geese. It is quite easily explored from roads north of Castle Douglas.
Carlingwark Loch, just outside Castle Douglas, is also worth visiting.
The National Trust owns the Threave marshes and has signposted
hides for bird-watchers.

At the western end of the region there is a group of lochs near
Stranraer which between them hold quite large numbers of dabbling
duck. Loch Ryan, the sea inlet to the north of the town, has a flock of
wintering Wigeon and also some sea duck. On the south coast there
are a number of estuaries, though mainly of minor importance, such
as Wigtown Bay, Fleet Bay and Rough Firth. These hold the usual
wader species, some duck and late wintering Pink-footed and Greylag
Geese.

The major wetland of the region is the north shore of the Solway
Firth. The south shore has already been covered under Cumbria; here
we are concerned with the stretch between Southerness and Annan.

North Solway   *Sheets 84 & 85 NY 0566*
On the north shore of the Solway Firth the major interest to wildfowl
and waders is found towards the outer part of the firth, between the
River Nith and the Lochar Water. This section of the coast is within
the Caerlaverock National Nature Reserve and also the overlapping
Wildfowl Trust Refuge. Together they contain the principal
wintering grounds of the Svalbard population of Barnacle Geese, a
roost and occasional feeding ground for thousands of Pink-footed
Geese, as well as large numbers of wintering waders and ducks. On
the west side of the River Nith is Kirkconnell Merse, the feeding
ground for large numbers of geese and a flock of Whooper Swans. At

the mouth of the river, also on the west side, is Carse Bay where flocks of wintering sea duck can be found. Further west still is Preston Merse, a final piece of saltmarsh before the rocky coast begins.

To reach Caerlaverock take the B725 out of Dumfries heading south for Glencaple. This road runs alongside the River Nith for several miles, giving excellent views across the river to Kirkconnell Merse and later over the mudflats and saltmarsh of the north end of the National Nature Reserve. There is a picnic site at the corner where the road turns inland. It is not permitted to walk on to the reserve but good views of waders on the mudflats can be had from here.

Continuing on the B725 one comes first to Caerlaverock Castle and then, down the next turning right (duly signposted), to the Wildfowl Trust Refuge. Parties accompanied by wardens are taken round at 1100 and 1400 throughout the winter and spring, visitors being taken to whichever of the many hides and observation towers gives the best view of the geese. The wintering Barnacle Geese can frequently be seen at very close quarters, as can a wide variety of duck, other geese, Whooper and Bewick's Swans, these last on some small pools also holding a collection of tame European wildfowl. Entrance is free for members of the Trust, while non-members pay a small fee.

The National Nature Reserve which adjoins and overlaps with the Wildfowl Trust Refuge cannot be entered without a permit from the Nature Conservancy Council and these are normally only given for some specified scientific purpose. One of the hides open to visitors is on the edge of the reserve and gives fine views out over the saltmarsh to the mudflats beyond, often teeming with waders.

Going east along the B725 takes one through Bankend and on past the mouth of the Lochar Water, from where quite good views over the Priestside mudflats can be had. Further east again, a number of small lanes lead down to the shore at Cummertrees, Powfoot and Annan and these sites are usually quite productive of waders.

Taking the A710 out of Dumfries on the west side of the Nith brings one past the inland side of Kirkconnell Merse and then to lanes leading to Carse Bay and Southerness, and finally a view from the side of a hill out over Preston Merse.

WILDFOWL

Whooper Swan	<100
Bewick's Swan	<100

Pink-footed Goose	2500– 5000
Barnacle Goose	5000–10000
Shelduck	250– 500
Mallard	500– 1000
Teal	100– 500
Wigeon	500– 1000
Pintail	500– 1000

Also: Mute Swan, Greylag Goose (100–250), Gadwall, Pochard, Tufted Duck, Goldeneye
The flock of Whooper Swans at Kirkconnell reaches about 80–100.

WADERS

Oystercatcher	10000+
Ringed Plover	500– 1000
Golden Plover	2500– 5000
Grey Plover	100– 250
Lapwing	5000–10000
Turnstone	250– 500
Dunlin	5000–10000
Knot	5000–10000
Redshank	2500– 5000
Bar-tailed Godwit	1000– 2500
Curlew	2500– 5000

Also: Purple Sandpiper, Spotted Redshank, Greenshank, Black-tailed Godwit, Whimbrel
Other birds: raptors
Easily the most important estuary in Scotland for waders, with Oystercatchers totalling more than 10% of the British population, and Ringed Plover, Knot and Bar-tailed Godwit over 5%. The Pintail numbers are the largest in Scotland.

FIFE

The region of Fife forms a promontory jutting out between the Firths of Forth and Tay. The latter is dealt with under Tayside. One other estuary lies within Fife, that of the River Eden, which is dealt with below, otherwise the coast is not of great interest. Inland there are two sites important to wildfowl, Cameron Reservoir, south of St Andrews, and Kilconquhar Loch, close to the Forth. Other waters are mostly very small and of only slight interest.

Cameron Reservoir
Only 40 ha (100 acres) in extent, Cameron Reservoir is used by a wide variety of ducks and by large numbers of roosting geese. It lies in a sheltered valley with well-grown plantations on either bank, about 6.5 km (4 miles) south-south-west from St Andrews. It is situated just east of the A915 (St Andrews to Leven) and is reached down a signposted lane. The water-keeper's cottage is beside the dam and permission to enter must be sought. The geese can usually be found feeding in the farmland down the valley to the east of the reservoir.

WILDFOWL

Pink-footed Goose	1000–2500
Greylag Goose	100– 250
Mallard	250– 500
Teal	100– 250
Wigeon	100– 250
Pochard	100– 250
Tufted Duck	100– 250
Goldeneye	<100

Also: Whooper Swan, Mute Swan, Gadwall, Pintail, Shoveler, Goosander

Eden Estuary
The estuary of the Eden is good for wildfowl and waders and has the added interest of sporadic visits by large numbers of sea ducks. The latter seem to spend most of their time on the sea off Tentsmuir Point at the mouth of the Firth of Tay but observations of large numbers of Scoters and Eiders off the Eden estuary are sufficiently frequent to suggest that they come south for shelter and perhaps food for periods of each winter.

Only the south side of the estuary is accessible as the Leuchars Air Force base occupies the northern bank. There is no evidence, however, that anyone objects to bird-watchers on the southern shore apparently staring at the airfield through telescopes or binoculars.

The birds of the estuary are remarkably tolerant of the almost continuous disturbance from low-flying jets.

The first observation point is at Guardbridge where the A919 to Leuchars crosses the head of the estuary. Then, travelling along the A91 towards St Andrews, one gets good views out over the estuary which can be improved by walking down one or two small tracks to the shore. On entering St Andrews, turn left down a road which runs on the east (seaward) side of the golf courses to Out Head and Shelly Point. One can walk round the shore westwards from here to overlook the estuary again, or look seawards for the flocks of sea ducks.

WILDFOWL

Shelduck	500–1000
Mallard	100– 250
Teal	250– 500
Wigeon	500–1000
Pintail	<100
Eider	250– 500
Scoter	1000–5000

Also: Pink-footed Goose (100–250), Goldeneye, Velvet Scoter and Long-tailed Duck (sporadic)

WADERS

Oystercatcher	2500–5000
Grey Plover	100– 250
Black-tailed Godwit	100– 250
Bar-tailed Godwit	1000–2500
Dunlin	2500–5000
Knot	1000–2500
Redshank	1000–2500

Also: Ringed Plover (100–250), Golden Plover (100–250), Turnstone, Sanderling

Kilconquhar Loch *Sheet 59 NO 4902*

Covering about 55 ha (135 acres) and no more than 2 m (6 ft) deep, Kilconquhar Loch is a rich water with plenty of submerged and emergent vegetation. Seven or eight species of wildfowl breed and it is noted as a late summer passage locality for Little Gulls which can number several hundreds. Wintering duck are numerous, especially Mallard and diving ducks, while Greylags use the water as a roost, feeding in the neighbouring fields.

Virtually the whole lock can be seen very well from the B941 which runs past the north and west sides through the village of Kilconquhar.

WILDFOWL

Greylag Goose	500–1000
Mallard	1000–2500
Teal	100– 250
Gadwall	100– 250
Pochard	500–1000
Tufted Duck	250– 500
Goldeneye	100– 250

Also: Mute Swan, Wigeon, Shoveler (100–250)
Mallard numbers are very high for such a relatively small water, and this is one of the larger flocks of Gadwall in the country.

GRAMPIAN _____

The north-east region of Scotland runs back into the highlands which are devoid of important wetlands, but the lowland plain and coast of Banff, Aberdeen and Kincardine are better off. On the north coast there are no proper estuaries, though the mouth of the Spey attracts small numbers of dabbling ducks, together with some sea ducks. Some miles to the west not far from Elgin, is Loch Spynie. This is an attractive loch holding a wide variety of dabling and diving duck and also acting as a roost for up to 1,000 Greylag Geese. Loch Park, rather further inland, near Dufftown, is noted for an autumn flock of Whooper Swans. The real gems of the region are, however, on the east coast, at the Loch of Strathbeg, between Peterhead and Frazerburgh, and the Ythan Estuary by Newburgh. These two are detailed below.

The Loch of Skene, a few miles inland from Aberdeen, and the Lochs of Davan and Kinord, further up the Dee valley, all attract good numbers of dabbling and diving duck, while Skene has a Greylag roost, often topping 1,500. Further Greylags are found roosting on floodwater and shallows in the Dee valley.

The southern part of the region has no inland waters of any size nor estuaries, though small numbers of sea duck can be found in some of the bays.

Loch of Strathbeg   *Sheet 30 NK 0759*

Up in the extreme north-east of the region, between Peterhead and Frazerburgh, Strathbeg is one of the most important waterfowl haunts in Scotland, indeed in Britain. It lies only 1 km (0.5 mile) from the sea, which greatly increases its attractiveness to migrants coming in from Iceland or Scandinavia, and is both large—200 ha (490 acres)—and shallow—mean depth 1.5 m (5 ft). It is a dune slack pool on a grand scale, the largest in the country, and is surrounded by calcareous dunes, making the water eutrophic, while run-off streams from adjacent farmland add to the nutrient levels of the water. Although much of the shore is stony and lacks emergent vegetation, there are extensive *Phragmites* beds at the north end and the submerged vegetation and rich invertebrate life provide a plentiful supply of food for a wide variety of duck. The loch is also used as a roost by very substantial numbers of Greylag and Pink-footed Geese, especially in the autumn, which is when the Whooper Swan flock is at its highest (often the largest flock in the country). A handful of Bewick's Swans are regular—their most northerly haunt in Britain.

The loch was recently made an RSPB reserve by arrangement with the owners, and a warden will escort visitors who must, however, have previously obtained a permit from him for a small fee (apply to: The Lythe, Crimongate, Frazerburgh). Apart from permit visits, good views of the southern half of the loch can be obtained from the unclassified road which passes close to the loch. This road leaves the A952 (Peterhead to Frazerburgh) between Blackhill and Crimond and runs down to the sea.

WILDFOWL

Mute Swan	250– 500
Whooper Swan	250– 500
Greylag Goose	2500–5000
Pink-footed Goose	2500–5000

Mallard	500–1000
Teal	100– 250
Wigeon	500–1000
Pochard	500–1000
Tufted Duck	500–1000
Goldeneye	250– 500

Also: Bewick's Swans, Shelduck, Goosander
Mallard were formerly very much more common, with peaks of 8,000 about 20 years ago. The reasons for this steep decline are not fully understood.
Other birds: breeding Eiders and grebes, passage waders
At its peak the Whooper Swan flock is perhaps 15% of the British wintering population. Only Lochs Harray, Stenness, Orkney, and Leven hold more Tufted Duck in Britain, while the latter holds equal numbers of Goldeneye, making these the two largest freshwater flocks in the country.

Ythan Estuary   *Sheet 38 NK 0026*
The estuary of the River Ythan is nearly 4.8 km (3 miles) long but only averages 0.4 km (0.25 mile) wide. This shape precludes very large numbers of birds but there is an excellent variety of wildfowl and waders, nearly always within close viewing distance. The estuary covers about 200 ha (500 acres). Adjacent to it are the extensive dunes of the Sands of Forvie, a National Nature Reserve, the breeding place of about 2,000 pairs of Eider Ducks as well as Sandwich and other terns.

Three small lochs, to the north and east of the estuary, also hold some ducks and more often than not act as the roosts of very large numbers of Greylag and Pink-footed Geese, though these do use the estuary also.

At Newburgh, on the west bank of the estuary, is the Culterty Field Station of Aberdeen University where some fine long-term research has been carried out on the birds of the area and whose presence accounts for the multi-coloured wing-tags and rings worn by many of the Eiders and Shelducks in the estuary.

Newburgh stands off the A975 to Peterhead, a turning off the A92 (Aberdeen to Frazerburgh) about 19 km (12 miles) north of Aberdeen. Just after passing through the village, the road skirts the western shore of the estuary, then crosses it on a bridge before running up the east bank. Excellent views can be obtained all along the road, one of the favoured duck and wader feeding areas being the Sleek of Tarty, an arm of the estuary on the west side just north of the bridge. Continuing along the A975 one comes to a right turn, the B9003 to Collieston; Cotehill Loch is a short way down here on the right, and Sand Loch is further on close to Collieston village. Back on the A975, Meikle Loch is on the left after about another mile and is approached down a short track just before a minor crossroads.

WILDFOWL (Ythan estuary and nearby lochs)

Whooper Swan	100– 250
Pink-footed Goose	5000–10000
Greylag Goose	2500– 5000
Mallard	500– 1000
Teal	100– 250
Wigeon	500– 1000
Goldeneye	<100
Eider	1000– 2500
Long-tailed Duck	<100
Red-breasted Merganser	<100

Also: Pochard, Tufted Duck, Mute Swan

WADERS

Oystercatcher	250– 500
Golden Plover	1000–2500
Lapwing	500–1000
Turnstone	<100
Dunlin	250– 500
Redshank	500–1000

Also: Ringed Plover (100–250), Knot, Curlew
Other birds: terns, skuas, seabirds

HIGHLAND _____

The major wetlands of the Highland region are in the east where the firths of Moray, Beauly, Cromarty and Dornoch between them provide a wealth of good habitat. Close by is the small estuary of Loch Fleet and the freshwater Loch Eye. Elsewhere, although the region has an enormous coastline, estuaries are mostly small and not too productive, lochs are oligotrophic and only the more sheltered inlets and bays hold typical sea ducks such as Eiders, Long-tailed Ducks and Mergansers.

Beauly Firth and Inner Moray Firth
Sheets 26 & 27, NH 6047 & NH 6949

The innermost part of the Moray Firth, called the Beauly Firth, has extensive areas of saltmarsh on the south side, with large expanses of exposed mud and sand at low water. Further out it becomes broader and deeper with less mudflat area, except for Munlochy Bay on the north side and Longman on the south. Both ducks and waders are present in considerable diversity and numbers, while Pinkfeet and Greylags roost in the Beauly Firth and in Munlochy Bay, particularly in the autumn and spring. The Beauly Firth is also the summer home of a flock of moulting Canada Geese which ringing has shown undertake a moult migration from Yorkshire. Flocks of sea ducks, especially the two sawbills, Red-breasted Merganser and Goosander, can be found offshore.

The Beauly Firth lies to the west of Inverness, separated from the inner Moray Firth by the narrowing at Kessoch. The south side of the firth can be seen from the A9 (Inverness to Beauly). There are convenient lay-bys along the road as far as Lentran Station. Continuing through Beauly on the A9 heading north, turn right at Muir of Ord on to the A832 towards Fortrose; turn right again off this road on to lanes leading to Redcastle, then along the north shore of the firth to North Kessoch, with excellent views at several points.

The south side of the inner Moray Firth can be seen well from a minor road running parallel with the A96 (Inverness to Nairn). It leaves the A96 just after the junction with the A9 and runs along the shore past Longman Bay, one of the best areas. Further along the A96, turn left on to the B9039 (Ardersier) at Newton for further views.

To reach the north shore one can either drive round on the A9

through Beauly, then on to the A832 for Fortrose, or take the Kessoch
ferry from Inverness, saving over 20 miles. From North Kessoch take
the A9161 for Munlochy at the head of the bay, then continue on the
A832 which comes close to the shore between Avoch and Fortrose.

WILDFOWL (Beauly Firth)

Mute Swan	<100
Whooper Swan	<100
Pink-footed Goose	250– 500
Greylag Goose	500–1000
Shelduck	<100
Mallard	500–1000
Teal	250– 500
Wigeon	500–1000
Pintail	<100
Tufted Duck	<100
Goldeneye	<100
Red-breasted	
Merganser	100– 250
Goosander	500–1000

WADERS (Beauly Firth)

Oystercatcher	250– 500
Lapwing	500–1000
Dunlin	250– 500
Redshank	500–1000
Bar-tailed Godwit	100– 250
Curlew	250– 500

Also: Turnstone, Knot, Black-tailed Godwit

WILDFOWL (Inner Moray Firth)

Mute Swan	<100
Pink-footed Goose	250– 500
Greylag Goose	500–1000
Shelduck	250– 500
Mallard	250– 500
Teal	250– 500
Wigeon	1000–2500

Pintail	100–250
Red-breasted Merganser	<100

Also: Goldeneye, Goosander

WADERS (Inner Moray Firth)

Oystercatcher	2500–5000
Ringed Plover	100– 250
Turnstone	100– 250
Dunlin	2500–5000
Knot	2500–5000
Redshank	1000–2500
Bar-tailed Godwit	1000–2500
Curlew	500–1000

Also: Lapwing (500–1,000), Purple Sandpiper, Sanderling

Cromarty Firth
Sheets 21 & 26 NH 6868

The Cromarty Firth is about 24 km (15 miles) long and varies considerably in width, opening out into some large shallow bays. The most important bird haunts are at the head of the estuary near the town of Dingwall; Udale Bay towards the mouth on the south side, and the three bays of Alness, Dalmore and Nigg on the north side. An oil refinery is now being built at Nigg and other works are threatened. Access may no longer be possible to all areas.

Roads run along the greater part of both shores. On the south side the B9163 (Cononbridge to Cromarty) gives excellent views over the head of the estuary and Udale Bay. The A9 (Dingwall to Alness) road stays close to the north shore until Alness, then take the B817 (Alness-Invergordon-Kilmuir) which continues along the shore up the west side of Nigg Bay. Turn back on to the A9, then immediately right again to Nigg to see the east side of the bay.

WILDFOWL

Mute Swan	100– 250
Whooper Swan	100– 250
Pink-footed Goose	500–1000
Greylag Goose	250– 500
Shelduck	250– 500
Mallard	500–1000

Teal	500– 1000
Wigeon	5000–10000
Goldeneye	500– 1000
Red-breasted	
Merganser	100– 250

WADERS

Oystercatcher	1000–2500
Ringed Plover	100– 250
Lapwing	1000–2500
Turnstone	<100
Dunlin	1000–2500
Knot	1000–2500
Redshank	1000–2500
Bar-tailed Godwit	500–1000
Curlew	500–1000

Also: Golden Plover, Greenshank, Black-tailed Godwit
The peak Wigeon numbers are over 5% of the British total; Whooper
Swans are about 10%.

Dornoch Firth and Loch Eye   *Sheet 21 NH 7686 & NH 8380*
The Dornoch Firth is rather smaller than the Cromarty but is still
very important for ducks, though less so for waders. The best areas
are on the south side between Edderton and Tain, with the Skibo Inlet
the major worthwhile site on the north shore.

About 6.5 km (4 miles) to the south of the Dornoch Firth is Loch
Eye, a 360 ha (890 acre) very shallow water, with a mean depth of
only 1.2 m (4 ft). Much of the shore is bare but there is swamp and fen
at the east end, while the underwater vegetation is particularly
diverse. The loch is very attractive to ducks and swans and is also used
as a goose roost. There is much movement between the estuary and
the loch.

The A9 runs along the south shore of the Dornoch Firth from Tain
to its head at Bonar Bridge, then back along the north shore as far as
Whiteface. The stretch from Tain Bay west to Meikle Ferry is
excellent for ducks, with Edderton Sands, slightly further west,
nearly as good. Both can be seen from the A9 or from the track leading
to the ferry. On the north side, Skibo Inlet is reached by turning off
the A9 at Whiteface or at Clashmore and going to the end of the
respective lanes.

Loch Eye can be reached by turning east in Tain on to an unclassified road heading for Portmahomack, then taking the second right and right again to bring one to the west end of the loch.

WILDFOWL (Dornoch)

Mute Swan	<100
Shelduck	100– 250
Mallard	250– 500
Teal	500–1000
Wigeon	2500–5000
Pintail	100– 250
Scaup	100– 250
Red-breasted Merganser	<100

Also: Goldeneye (100–250), Eider

WADERS (Dornoch)

Oystercatcher	250–500
Golden Plover	100–250
Lapwing	250–500
Turnstone	<100
Dunlin	250–500
Knot	100–250
Redshank	100–250

Also: Ringed Plover, Grey Plover, Purple Sandpiper

WILDFOWL (Loch Eye)

Mute Swan	100– 250
Whooper Swan	100– 250
Greylag Goose	1000–2500
Mallard	100– 250
Teal	100– 500
Wigeon	100– 500

Also: Pochard, Tufted Duck

Loch Fleet   *Sheet 21 NH 8096*
Situated on the east coast just north of the Dornoch Firth, Loch Fleet is an almost completely enclosed shallow tidal basin of sandflats and is

virtually dry at low water. Beyond it lies an extensive alder carr which provides additional good feeding grounds for ducks.

The main A9 trunk road to Wick skirts the western end, first giving an excellent overall view as one comes down the hill from the south. Near the bottom of the hill an unclassified road leaves to the right and follows the southern shore to Skelbo. Carrying on along this road brings one to Embo on the coast and overlooking an area of shallow sea on which flocks of Common and Velvet Scoters can be seen in the winter months. The upper part of Loch Fleet is visible from the A9, as is a freshwater pool on the left-hand side of the road as it crosses an old causeway which divides the estuary proper from the alder carr.

WILDFOWL

Whooper Swan	<100
Shelduck	100– 250
Mallard	250– 500
Teal	100– 250
Wigeon	500–1000
Goldeneye	<100
Red-breasted Merganser	<100
Eider	100– 250

Also: Long-tailed Duck

WADERS

Oystercatcher	500–1000
Knot	100– 250
Redshank	100– 250
Curlew	100– 250

Also: Ringed Plover, Lapwing (100–250), Dunlin, Purple Sandpiper, Bar-tailed Godwit

LOTHIANS _____

The coastline of the Lothians Region covers almost the entire southern side of the Firth of Forth, with only the head of the estuary in the Central Region, but this is covered here for convenience. This deep inlet, although heavily industrialized along several sections, including some former rich mudflats, still holds large numbers of waterfowl. The most important duck concentration is just off the docks of east Edinburgh where huge flocks of sea ducks concentrate round the outfalls of Edinburgh's sewage. Both upstream and downstream from Edinburgh there are good wildfowl and wader areas; at Tullibody and Grangemouth to the west, and Aberlady, Gullane Bay and Tyninghame Estuary to the east.

Inland, several hill reservoirs have been constructed, many of which are used by Greylag and Pink-footed Geese as roosts, but only one, Gladhouse Reservoir, is of real importance to ducks as well. Others, including Cobbinshaw, Harperrig, Threipmuir and Rosebery, carry only small numbers of the commoner species.

Finally, actually within the city of Edinburgh is Duddingston Loch, a unique duck roost dealt with below.

Duddingston Loch   *Sheet 66 NT 2873*
Lying within Holyrood Park, close to the centre of Edinburgh, this 8 ha (20 acre) loch with an adjoining reedbed carries astonishing numbers of Pochard, plus smaller numbers of a few other species. Clearly such a tiny loch cannot provide the food for several thousand ducks and it seems that the bulk of them flight out each evening to feed in the Forth.

Although direct access to the loch is not allowed it can, in fact, be seen at close quarters from within the Park, particularly from the road running through it.

WILDFOWL

Greylag Goose	<100
Mallard	100– 250
Teal	<100
Pochard	5000–10000

| Tufted Duck | 250–500 |
| Scaup | <100 |

Easily the largest flock of Pochard in the country, and about 15% of the British wintering population.

Firth of Forth   *Sheets 58, 65, 66 & 67*

Going from west to east along the south side of the firth, one starts at Tullibody Island (NJ 8792) opposite Alloa. This area holds good numbers of Shelduck and a variety of waders. Viewing is from the main A905 (Stirling to Falkirk) as it passes close to the shore at Mains of Throsk, and from the B906 to South Alloa, a turning to the left just beyond Mains of Throsk.

The next site is around Grangemouth which, despite heavy industrialization, still manages to hold important numbers of Shelduck and waders. Access has changed in recent years and is changing still as more industry moves in, so that all that can really be suggested is to make for the Grangemouth docks area and for Longannet Point at its furthest extremity. Other views should be obtained from Skinflats, a small village just west of Grangemouth and reached down a turning off the A905. Paths lead from the village to the shore.

The mussel beds off Musselburgh and Seafield, in the eastern districts of Edinburgh, support some of the largest sea-duck flocks in the country. The birds also feed on the sewage effluent of the city, which presumably contributes also to the well-being of the mussels. The very recent completion of a sewage treatment works will have some effect—so far not known—on the ducks which may well find less food than hitherto and so be forced to move elsewhere.

One of the best observation points is at Seafield where it is possible to reach the shore; also from the A199 (Portobello to Musselburgh) and from Leith Docks. The birds move to and fro depending on the tide.

The first large bay east of Edinburgh is Aberlady Bay, a Local Nature Reserve covering about 570 ha (1,400 acres) of dunes and mudflats. Wildfowl and waders occur here in good numbers and variety, with the added interest of sea ducks and roosting Pinkfeet. The geese come particularly late in the winter after the end of the shooting season. The A198 (Edinburgh to North Berwick) passes the head of the bay and there is unrestricted access for walkers down either side.

Large flocks of sea ducks also congregate off Gullane Bay, just to the east of Aberlady. These can be observed by continuing the walk round the east side of the bay and round the headland, or by walking (with care) across Gullane Golf Course from a little further along the A198.

Finally, and really out of the Forth and facing the North Sea, is Tyninghame Estuary just north of Dunbar. This carries a good mixture of estuarine and sea ducks and also waders. Paths lead from the A198 just north of its junction with the A1, and from the A1087 just west of Dunbar.

WILDFOWL (Inner Firth above Edinburgh)

Whooper Swan	<100
Shelduck	1000–2500
Mallard	500–1000
Teal	500–1000
Wigeon	100– 500
Pintail	<100
Goldeneye	250– 500
Red-breasted Merganser	<100

WILDFOWL (Leith–Musselburgh)

Scaup	10000–25000
Goldeneye	2500– 5000
Common Scoter	500– 1000
Eider	5000–10000
Longtail	100– 250
Red-breasted Merganser	<100

Also: Velvet Scoter
Easily the largest Scaup flock in the country, up to 75% of the total, but there are signs of a recent sharp decrease to under 5,000.

WILDFOWL (Aberlady Bay)

Pink-footed Goose	1000–2500
Whooper Swan	<100
Shelduck	100– 250
Wigeon	250– 500
Eider	100– 500
Common Scoter	100– 250

Also: Long-tailed Duck

WILDFOWL (Gullane Bay)

Eider	500–1000
Common Scoter	1000–2500
Velvet Scoter	100– 250
Long-tailed Duck	<100
Red-breasted Merganser	<100

WILDFOWL (Tyninghame Estuary)

Mute Swan	<100
Shelduck	100–250
Mallard	250–500
Teal	100–250
Wigeon	250–500
Goldeneye	<100
Eider	100–250
Common Scoter	<100

Also: Pink-footed Goose (100–250), Red-breasted Merganser, Goosander

WADERS (whole Firth of Forth)

Oystercatcher	5000+
Ringed Plover	250– 500
Golden Plover	500–1000
Grey Plover	100– 250
Lapwing	1000–2500
Turnstone	500–1000
Dunlin	10000+
Knot	10000+
Sanderling	<100

Redshank	2500–5000
Purple Sandpiper	100– 250
Bar-tailed Godwit	1000–2500
Curlew	1000–2500

Also: Curlew Sandpiper, Greenshank, Black-tailed Godwit, Whimbrel
The overall numbers of sea ducks are not exceeded anywhere else in
Britain. Some of the wader species are significant in Scottish terms, par-
ticularly Turnstone, Knot, Redshank and Bar-tailed Godwit.

Gladhouse Reservoir   *Sheet 66 NT 3054*

Of all the reservoirs in the Moorfoot Hills behind Edinburgh this is
the largest, 305 ha (750 acres), and favourite of the ducks. It is
relatively shallow but has little marginal vegetation. As well as ducks
it is a very important Pink-footed Goose roost.

The reservoir is best approached from Edinburgh down the A7
road to Galashiels. Just after Gorebridge turn right on to the B6372.
Take the fourth on the left past the dam of Rosebery reservoir and up
its east side, and then round the north side of Gladhouse for a view
over most of the water. Access off the road is not permitted.

WILDFOWL

Greylag Goose	<100
Pink-footed Goose	2500–5000
Mallard	250– 500
Teal	100– 500
Wigeon	100– 250
Tufted Duck	100– 250
Goldeneye	<100
Goosander	<100

ORKNEY _____

This group of islands lying across the Pentland Firth from the north-
east tip of Scotland contains rather few good freshwater wetlands as
most of the lochs are too small or too disturbed. The Loch of Harray is

an exception, as is its close neighbour, the saltwater Loch of Stenness. These are dealt with below. Scapa Flow carries good numbers of waders and sea ducks.

Lochs of Harray and Stenness — *Sheet 6 HY 3013*

The total area of these two lochs is about 1,400 ha (4,000 acres). Stenness is joined to the sea by a narrow tidal channel and linked with Harray by culverts. Because of these connections the two lochs show a unique gradation from eutrophic fresh water at the head of Harray to salt water at the outlet of Stenness. The stony shores of both lochs reduce their attraction to dabbling ducks, but diving ducks on Harray and sea ducks on Stenness both find conditions to suit them. Mute and Whooper Swans also winter in important numbers.

The lochs lie on the west side of the mainland of Orkney, to the north of the A965 (Kirkwall to Stromness) about ten miles from Kirkwall. The B9055 runs between them giving views of and access to both.

WILDFOWL (Loch of Harray)

Mute Swan	100– 250
Greylag Goose	100– 250
Mallard	100– 250
Wigeon	500–1000
Pochard	1000–2500
Tufted Duck	1000–2500
Scaup	100– 250
Goldeneye	100– 250

Also: Whooper Swan, Teal, Red-breasted Merganser

WILDFOWL (Loch of Stenness)

Mute Swan	100–250
Mallard	100–250
Wigeon	250–500
Tufted Duck	100–250
Goldeneye	100–250
Red-breasted Merganser	<100

Also: Whooper Swan, Teal (100–250), Pochard, Scaup
The largest flock of Tufted Duck and the second largest flock of Pochard in the country.

OUTER HEBRIDES _____

The Outer Isles, taken together, hold quite large numbers of waterfowl but the flocks, like the land itself, are so fragmented as to make proper assessment difficult. The Long Island of Lewis and Harris is generally not productive, being almost entirely acidic in both rocks and water. Small numbers of a variety of duck species occur around Broad Bay beside Stornoway.

The Sound of Harris and its many islands hold more birds, though still not in large flocks. Greylag Geese are resident on the Uists and Benbecula, while wintering Barnacle Geese can be found on several islands. The largest flocks occur on the Monachs, the Shiants and in the Sound of Harris. Sea ducks winter in the sheltered waters between the islands but the status of most species is not properly known. There is a large population of Mute Swans on the Uists and Benbecula, and Whooper Swans winter.

SHETLAND _____

This northern archipelago of islands is very well known for its breeding sea birds, but apart from the resident Eider, which is very common, ducks are not plentiful, while waders are restricted to small numbers breeding, including Whimbrel, and a very few at other times of year. Some of the lochs do carry a variety of wintering duck but only rarely does any one species top 100 on a single water. Sea duck winter in some areas but there are few good counts. Whooper Swans pass through on passage from Iceland and some stay to winter, particularly on Loch Spiggie in the south of the mainland.

STRATHCLYDE _____

Despite its great size, the region of Strathclyde has few wetlands of real importance. The Firth of Clyde holds quite good numbers of waders and ducks if taken as a whole but no one locality is of tremendous interest. Most of the long arms of the firth, like the other fjord-like sea lochs of the Argyll coast, support small numbers of Goldeneye and Mergansers but not much else. Greylag Geese occur in a number of localities scattered through the region and there are Greenland Whitefronts at various places on the Mull of Kintyre and to the north. Just one of the many islands of Argyll, the island of Islay, is the home of over two-thirds of the Greenland population of Barnacle Geese, and this is dealt with in detail below.

Inland waters are quite numerous but the majority are at a high altitude or oligotrophic or both. An exception is Castle Semple Loch in what used to be Renfrewshire, and this is covered below. There is also a fine wetland area at the south-east corner of Loch Lomond, the Endrick Mouth National Nature Reserve, which attracts many duck, Greylag Geese and Whooper Swans. However access is strictly limited.

Castle Semple Loch (Lochwinnoch)   *Sheet 63 NS 3659*
Despite its size—over 2.4 km (1.5 miles) long by up to 400 m (400 yds) wide—this loch is very shallow, less than 1.5 m (5 ft) deep, and rich in aquatic plants and animals. With such a good food supply it is not surprising that both numbers and variety of wildfowl are large.

Access arrangements are still being organised by the RSPB who recently acquired the loch as a reserve, but it is possible to obtain good views from the southern end, although a railway running the full length of the eastern side restricts other views as well as access. The A737 (Glasgow to Irvine) passes the eastern side of the loch, and at the southern end the A760 leaves for Largs. Just after crossing the two river channels an unclassified road leaves the A760 on the right for the town of Lochwinnoch. Views of the loch may be had from here and from further up the west side following a lane out of Lochwinnoch running parallel with the railway on that side and then crossing underneath it.

WILDFOWL

Mute Swan	<100
Whooper Swan	<100
Greylag Goose	100– 500
Mallard	250– 500
Teal	100– 250
Wigeon	250– 500
Pochard	500–1000
Tufted Duck	500–1000
Goldeneye	<100

Islay   *Sheet 60 NR 3070*

The Island of Islay is the southernmost of the Inner Hebrides, lying about 32 km (20 miles) off the mainland coast of the Mull of Kintyre and not much further from the coast of Northern Ireland. A large island, nearly 32 km (20 miles) across, it has a deep indentation on the south side, Loch Indaal, and a smaller one, Loch Gruinart, on the north. These are the actual wetlands of this island and are not really important for anything except roosting Barnacle Geese and a flock of Scaup. However the Barnacle Geese could not survive without them. The geese spread out to feed over the surrounding farmland and directions for finding them are hardly necessary. They are present between late October and mid-April with the largest concentrations on the fields adjacent to Loch Gruinart, particularly the flats at its head, and along the Ardnave Peninsula to the west. Greenland White-fronted Geese are also plentiful on the island and are found scattered over most of the farmland areas in quite small flocks. A small but regular flock of Greylags occurs in the Bridgend area, while other geese, including Snow, Canada, Pinkfoot and Brent, are often seen singly among the larger flocks of Whitefronts or Barnacles.

Small numbers of the commoner dabbling ducks are found, especially round the inner shores of Loch Indaal, as are flocks of waders, including wintering Bar-tailed Godwits. Off the tiny harbour of Bowmore there is a wintering flock of Scaup, the second largest in the country, while Eiders are also common in the Bay. Eiders and Red-breasted Mergansers are found scattered round all the island coasts.

Islay is reached by two car ferries from West Loch Tarbert on the Mull of Kintyre or by plane from Glasgow. Full details of these and of

accommodation on the island can be obtained from the Islay, Jura and
Colonsay Tourist Association, Bowmore, Islay.

While this book is limited to wetlands, it is nevertheless worth
pointing out that the bird life of Islay is as rich and diverse as almost
anywhere in the country and a tally of 100 species on the island is not
too difficult to achieve during a winter week.

WILDFOWL

Whooper Swan	<100
Greenland Whitefront	2500–5000
Barnacle Goose	20000+
Greylag Goose	<100
Shelduck	<100
Mallard	100– 250
Teal	250– 500
Wigeon	250– 500
Scaup	1000–2500
Eider	500–1000

WADERS

Oystercatcher	100– 250
Ringed Plover	<100
Golden Plover	100– 250
Lapwing	1000–2500
Turnstone	<100
Dunlin	100– 250
Bar-tailed Godwit	250– 500
Redshank	100– 250
Curlew	500–1000

Also: Knot, Purple Sandpiper

The Barnacle Geese represent up to 75% of the total Greenland breeding
population; the Greenland Whitefronts are about 30% of their
population. The Scaup flock is the second largest in the country.

TAYSIDE _____

Angus, Kinross and Perth make up the region of Tayside and between them contain several very important waterfowl haunts. The coast of the old county of Angus has the potentially very good estuary of Montrose Basin which, now that shooting disturbance is to be controlled, should attract many more birds. The coastline south to the mouth of the Firth of Tay has no major indentation but some of the shallower bays contain Eiders and other sea ducks.

The Firth of Tay is the sole major estuary in this region and is shared with Fife. It is in fact so large as to have provided some problems with counting its birds, especially the ducks. Inland there are several very attractive lochs and reservoirs, often the more attractive for being in small groups so that the ducks and roosting geese have an alternative close by if disturbed off one water. In Angus there are the lochs of Rescobie and Balgavies, just east of Forfar, with Forfar Loch on the west side of the town still used but no longer so important as it once was. Just north and west from here are Lochs Kinnordy and Lintrathen—the one a partially drained natural water, the other a reservoir—both, in their different ways, of considerable importance. Down the Isla valley and into Perthshire, around Blairgowrie, one comes to a whole group of small lochs of more value to roosting Greylags than to duck, and this is also true of some lochs to the west and south-west of Perth at Carsebreck and Drummond. The great Lochs of Tay, Earn, Tummel and Rannoch carry only small numbers of the commoner duck but are too deep and oligotrophic to be of greater value.

Finally, in the tiny former county of Kinross is the finest loch of all, Loch Leven, with more breeding ducks than anywhere else in Britain, large flocks of wintering duck and thousands of geese.

Blairgowrie Lochs   *Sheet 53 NO 2042*
Between Coupar Angus and Blairgowrie and to the west of the latter town there are several small lochs, some shallow with fringing marsh, others in more steeply sided valleys. There are also two rivers, the Tay and the Isla, which join at Kinclaven. Within this area roosts an average November peak of about 9,000 Greylags, gradually dropping through the winter, although sometimes with a spring build-up. They roost at several sites, including most of the lochs,

selecting them according to disturbance and weather conditions, and also on the shingle banks in the River Tay, especially between Kinclaven and Caputh. They feed in the surrounding farmland, often very close to the road, especially round Meiklour, and along the Isla between there and Coupar Angus, and then up the Isla valley as far as Meigle. A drive round the roads and lanes of this area in the first half of November cannot fail to produce close views of many thousands of geese.

Some of the small lochs carry ducks, too, with Stormont, Marlee and Clunie being among the best, holding several hundred Mallard, Teal and Wigeon between them, with smaller numbers of Tufted Duck and Goldeneye. The rivers, too, have duck on them, especially Goldeneye, Red-breasted Merganser and Goosanders.

Curling Ponds, Carsebreck   *Sheet 58 NN 8610*

From Perth, the main A9 road runs south-west towards Dunblane and passes through some of the best goose-watching areas in Britain. The Earn valley between Forteviot and Dunning, and the area to the north between Methven and Kinkell Bridge, hold some of the largest flocks of Pinkfeet in the country, at least during the autumn. Further south-west the A9 passes through Blackford and then past two small ponds lying to the right of, and rather below, the road. On the right-hand side of the road there is a convenient lay-by overlooking them. From here it is possible to see Greylags feeding on the banks of one of the pools, also several hundred ducks—mainly Mallard, Teal, Wigeon, and Tufted duck—as well as Mute and Whooper Swans. In the fields around, and particularly on the flat fields adjoining the Allan Water near Greenloaning and Braco, and again on the south side of the A9 between Blackford and Greenloaming, can be found several thousand Pinkfeet and Greylags. Numbers are highest in November when peaks of 6,000 of each species have been recorded, with more regular counts of 3,000–5,000. The small ponds are the main roosts and the geese can be watched pouring into them as dusk falls. The land around is private and access to it is quite unnecessary.

Loch Leven   *Sheet 58 NO 1501*

This loch has the distinction of being the largest natural eutrophic water in the country, covering about 1,600 ha (3,900 acres). There are six islands of which the largest, St Serf's, has larger numbers of breeding ducks—mainly Tufted Duck and Mallard—than any other site in Britain. Smaller numbers of Wigeon, Shoveler, Gadwall and Shelduck also breed.

The loch is not very deep and there is rich feeding in it for very large numbers of wintering duck, while a flock of Whooper Swans, and several thousand each of Greylag and Pink-footed Geese roost on the water and feed in the surrounding farmland. For the latter it is also a very important autumn arrival point.

The best views of the loch can be had from the south side at Vane Farm on the B9097 which runs from junction 5 on the M90 (Edinburgh to Kinross) motorway to Balingry and Glenrothes. Vane Farm is an RSPB reserve with viewing facilities out over the loch to St Serf's Island, and there are often geese feeding in nearby fields. Further along the same road there is a public picnic site, again giving good views over the loch. Elsewhere access is not very good, and the water's edge can only be reached at Kirkgate Park, signposted from the centre of Kinross. The whole lake and shoreline is a National Nature Reserve and walking along the water's edge is not permitted.

WILDFOWL

Whooper Swan	100– 250
Greylag Goose	2500– 5000
Pink-footed Goose	5000–10000
Mallard	1000– 2500
Teal	250– 500
Wigeon	500– 1000
Shoveler	250– 500
Pochard	500– 1000
Tufted Duck	1000– 2500
Goldeneye	250– 500
Goosander	100– 250

Also: Mute Swan (100–250), Shelduck, Gadwall, Pintail
The second largest flock of Tufted Duck in the country, exceeded only by that on Lochs of Harray and Stenness, Orkney; and equal largest numbers of Goldeneye with Loch of Strathbeg.

Lochs of Lintrathen and Kinnordy
Sheets 53 & 54 NO 2855 Lintrathen, NO 3654 Kinnordy
This first pair of lochs in the old county of Angus differs markedly

from the following pair. Lintrathen, about 10 km (7 miles) west of Kirriemuir, is a reservoir of about 220 ha (545 acres), fairly deep towards the dam and the southern end but with considerable shallows and some fairly sheltered bays at the northern end. The Loch of Kinnordy is only 3.5 km (2 miles) west of Kirriemuir and covers about 65 ha (160 acres). It was formerly much larger but was partially drained last century and there now remains extensive and rich fen which is seasonally flooded, with some permanent water. Of the two, Lintrathen carries much larger numbers of wintering duck while Kinnordy is a centre for breeding duck and other birds. Both waters act as a roost for a large population of Greylag Geese which feed in the farmland to the south, and between the two lochs. There is considerable interchange between the two depending on local conditions of weather, food and disturbance. The RSPB has recently established a reserve on the Loch of Kinnordy.

The Loch of Lintrathen is more or less ringed by unclassified roads leading off the B951 (Kirriemuir to Glenisla) which passes the north side. Forestry plantations restrict the view of some areas but the important northern shallows can be overlooked from the east side from one lane and also approached very closely on this side by another lane. Access to the banks is not permitted and is in any case unnecessary in order to see most of the reservoir.

The Loch of Kinnordy is not quite so easy to see in its entirety as Loch of Lintrathen, but the same B951 road out of Kirriemuir heading west passes close on the south side. Much of the west end and its shallows and marsh can be readily seen from this road, while it is hoped that fairly soon the RSPB will be able to provide hides giving views over the eastern end which is hard to see at present.

WILDFOWL (Lintrathen)

Greylag Goose	500–1000
Whooper Swan	<100
Mallard	2500–5000
Teal	100– 250
Wigeon	100– 250
Pochard	100– 250
Tufted Duck	100– 250

Also: Shoveler, Goldeneye, Goosander
The largest number of Mallard in Scotland

WILDFOWL (Kinnordy)

Greylag Goose	1000–2500
Mallard	100– 500
Teal	<100
Shoveler	<100
Pochard	<100
Tufted Duck	<100

Lochs Rescobie and Balgavies   *Sheet 54 NO 5251*

These two attractive and fertile lochs lie just east of Forfar. They are
connected by a small stream and their combined area is 215 ha (530
acres), with Rescobie very much the larger. They are both rich in
nutrients and with much emergent and submerged vegetation. They
carry a good mixture of ducks and also act as a roost for Pinkfooted
and Greylag Geese. The latter feed in the general vicinity of the lochs
but the Pinkfeet usually flight out northwards to feed in the South Esk
valley near Brechin. The lochs have gained in importance in recent
years as Forfar Loch, on the opposite side of the town of Forfar, has
become increasingly used for recreation, particularly sailing. The
Scottish Wildlife Trust have a reserve on Loch Balgavies.

Roads run along the north and south sides of both lochs. Loch
Rescobie is best seen from the north side on the B9113 (Forfar to
Montrose), while the better views of Balgavies are from the south on
the A932 (Forfar to Friockheim) and from the unclassified road which
joins the A932 with the B9113 just east of the loch. There is no need to
leave the road.

WILDFOWL

Pink-footed Goose	1000–2500
Greylag Goose	500–1000
Mallard	250– 500
Wigeon	100– 250
Pochard	100– 250
Tufted Duck	100– 250

Also: Teal, Goldeneye

Montrose Basin

Almost completely landlocked, this estuary covers about 1,125 ha (2,800 acres) of which three-quarters is mudflats, the rest saltmarsh and channel. The mud is rich in *Hydrobia* and the area is capable of supporting very high numbers of duck and waders. Until recently, however, shooting pressure and disturbance have been very high and the full potential of this wetland has not been approached. Recent changes for the better should bring about a large decrease in disturbance and a corresponding increase in birds. Grey geese used to roost here in great numbers but, as elsewhere in Scotland, they have moved to more secure inland roosts and it remains to be seen whether they can be attracted back.

Observation of the basin is relatively easy with the A935 (Brechin to Montrose) running alongside the north shore, and the A934 (Forfar to Montrose) along the south side, then across the causeway and into the town of Montrose. On the west side an unclassified road joins the two main roads and gives good views, particularly of the south-west corner.

WILDFOWL

Mute Swan	100– 250
Greylag Goose	250– 500
Shelduck	250– 500
Mallard	100– 500
Wigeon	2500–5000
Pintail	<100
Eider	500–1000
Goldeneye	<100

WADERS

Oystercatcher	1000–2500
Ringed Plover	100– 250
Lapwing	250– 500
Dunlin	1000–2500
Knot	2500–5000
Redshank	1000–2500
Bar-tailed Godwit	100– 250
Curlew	500–1000

Also: Grey Plover, Golden Plover (100–250), and Turnstone (100–250)

Tay Estuary   *Sheets 54, 58 & 59 NO 3426*

This is one of the largest estuaries in the country, stretching back
nearly 48 km (30 miles) from Buddon Ness, on the north side at the
mouth, to Perth. It can be divided into two parts; the mouth between
Buddon Ness and Tentsmuir Point, outside Broughty Ferry and
Tayport, and the inner firth, above Dundee. The outer reaches are
most noted for their sea ducks, of which Eider is the most important.
Scaup were formerly common but are now much reduced. Smaller
numbers of Goldeneye and sawbills occur, the former particularly at
the sewer outfalls on the north shore.

Observing these birds is not easy as they often lie well offshore. On
the north bank the shore can be reached at Broughty Ferry off the
A930 (Dundee to Carnoustie). Observation here, especially at a
sewer outfall, can often be rewarding. On the south side much of the
shore is inaccessible, lying within the Tentsmuir National Nature
Reserve, although there is access to the reserve provided a permit is
obtained first from the Nature Conservancy Council (12 Hope
Terrace, Edinburgh 9). The track to the reserve leads past the
attractive Morton Lochs, off the B945 (Tayport to Leuchars).

The inner firth has very extensive mudflats on the northern side,
stretching from just west of Dundee to the narrowing of the estuary
at the junction with the River Earn. They are separated from the
shore for over half this length by a thick belt of *Phragmites* which runs
for about 13 km (8 miles) from near Kingoodie to beyond Errol,
forming one of the largest reedbeds in the country. Quite large
numbers of waders inhabit the mudflats but duck numbers seem
generally small although it is often supposed that the reeds conceal
considerable numbers. Pink-footed and Greylag Geese roost on the
inner firth but rarely in large numbers, preferring the small inland
lochs where they are protected from shooting. Only exceptionally do
really large numbers of geese now come there, though many years
ago they did, and regular totals of only a few thousand Pinkfeet and
up to 1,000 Greylag are all that can be expected.

The extensive reedbeds on the north side make the mudflats
difficult to see, although there are a number of access points to the
shore and even some tracks through to the mud. These should be
looked for off the B958 (Dundee to Errol) from which various lanes
and tracks turn off to the left, coming from Dundee. During the
autumn and winter wildfowling pressure is high and most of the
access points attract at least one shooter. On the south side the shore is
clear, with the unclassified road from Newburgh to Balmerino

giving excellent views out over the estuary as it is often 30 m (100 ft) or more above the water level. Unfortunately distances are usually great as the channel mostly follows the southern shore.

WILDFOWL (certainly incomplete)

Pink-footed Goose	2500–5000
Greylag Goose	500–1000
Mallard	1000–2500
Teal	500–1000

WADERS

Oystercatcher	1000–2500
Golden Plover	250– 500
Lapwing	500–1000
Dunlin	2500–5000
Knot	250– 500
Sanderling	100– 250
Redshank	1000–2500
Bar-tailed Godwit	500–1000
Curlew	250– 500

Also: Ringed Plover, Grey Plover, Turnstone

Index

Entries in Roman type indicate sites dealt with in full; those in italics are mentioned briefly.